THE DARK CLOUD

Navigating Cybersecurity in a Hyper-Connected Ecosystem

Jacob Alebiosu

The Dark Cloud: Navigating Cybersecurity in a Hyper-Connected Ecosystem

Table of contents

Preface

The world has moved beyond cables and satellites into a seamless cloud of infinite connectivity where every device every system and every individual is wired into a vast digital lattice. Yet in this vastness lurks a darkness one not born from lack but from misuse deception and vulnerability. I wrote The Dark Cloud not merely to expose the risks and realities of cyber insecurity but to build clarity for readers whether tech-savvy or not who must now face a world that is always online and always at risk.

Foreword

There has never been a more critical time to examine the delicate digital fabric binding societies economies governments and individuals. In the hyper-connected ecosystem we occupy cybersecurity is no longer the concern of corporations or intelligence communities alone. It is now the frontline of everyday life. The Dark Cloud captures this new reality with gripping clarity and profound insight. In a voice that is both accessible and authoritative he takes us through the evolution of digital vulnerabilities the manipulation of systems the exploitation of trust and the emergence of new digital threats in an age of convenience and speed.

Introduction

There was a time when cybersecurity was a backroom concern discussed only by engineers and analysts far removed from public discourse. Today cybersecurity headlines dominate global news not because the world has grown more curious but because it has become more vulnerable. More systems have gone online more data is being collected stored and sold and more activities from education to warfare have moved into the digital realm. This is not simply digital evolution it is digital dependence and dependence invites exploitation. This book was born out of the realization that we have crossed a point of no return. Devices now talk to each other without human intervention. Homes now respond to voices instead of switches. Vehicles are programmed rather than driven. The very environment in which we live has become intelligent and thus manipulable. Every connection every convenience every shortcut becomes an opportunity for attack. But this book is not about fear. It is about visibility. It is about understanding what lies behind the curtain of digital efficiency about knowing how data is tracked harvested and sometimes weaponized. It is about recognizing that every digital action leaves a footprint and that those footprints can lead to either progress or peril. In The Dark Cloud we will journey through the architecture of cyber threats. Not just the technologies but the motives the loopholes and the consequences. We will explore the dark web the human errors the automated vulnerabilities and the calculated moves of hackers and defenders alike. We will confront uncomfortable truths about the systems we trust and the behaviors we normalize. And we will build a mindset that does not panic in the face of digital danger but responds with clarity and control. You do not need to be a cybersecurity expert to understand this world. You only need to be aware and willing to see the threats that live in the conveniences you love. Because the most dangerous threat is the one you do not see and the safest future belongs to those who prepare for it. This transformation, while convenient, introduces unprecedented levels of exposure. Where once systems were isolated and hardened, they are now open and integrated. Devices from different manufacturers interact on shared platforms. APIs grant remote access. Cloud systems offer limitless storage and scalability, but they also invite new forms of infiltration. Each innovation removes friction but also reduces the boundaries that once protected digital environments. Cybersecurity is no longer the domain of IT departments alone. It is now a central concern for individuals, families, corporations, and nations. The risks are no longer confined to corporate espionage or high-profile breaches. They extend to stolen identities, manipulated data, hijacked medical devices, and altered infrastructure controls. Everything connected can be attacked. Every system built for efficiency can be used against itself. Modern attackers do not knock down doors. They study, mimic, inject, and wait. Their goal is not chaos alone, but access, leverage, and control. Unlike physical theft, cyber breaches often go unnoticed. Data is copied, not removed. Logs are altered. Access is escalating silently. The illusion of normalcy is maintained until consequences emerge in the form of drained accounts, disrupted systems, or public exposure. By the time victims become aware, the breach has often spread, replicated, and monetized.

Cyber threats are not random. They are deliberate, targeted, and intelligent. Today's attackers range from lone actors to organized crime networks, from rogue insiders to nation-states conducting digital espionage. They exploit gaps in design, misconfigurations, delayed patches, and most often, human behavior. A single moment of trust in a forged link can open a gateway. A file labeled as urgent can lead to total system compromise. The human layer remains the most exploited layer. People trust what looks familiar. They act under pressure. They click before thinking. They share without verifying. Attackers understand this and craft their methods accordingly. Social engineering remains one of the most effective attack vectors not because of technological superiority, but because of psychological manipulation. Awareness is the first defense, and yet it remains the most neglected.

True cybersecurity requires more than products. It requires culture, behavior, and understanding. Systems must be built for failure, not perfection. Organizations must prepare for compromise, not assume immunity. Every tool used in defense firewalls, endpoint protection, intrusion detection, multifactor authentication must be maintained, tested, and adapted. Threats change. Defenses must change faster. Cyber risk is not just a technical issue. It is economic, legal, ethical, and strategic. Breaches affect stock markets. Attacks on hospitals endanger lives. Tampered elections affect governments. Manipulated data destroys reputations. The impact is rarely contained. It ripples across systems, users, partners, and communities. Digital trust, once lost, is difficult to rebuild. The cost of unpreparedness is no longer measured only in dollars, but in confidence and stability. Digital identity is now fragmented across dozens of platforms.

From social media to banking portals, a user's presence is scattered in tokens, cookies, biometric keys, and behavioral patterns.

Chapter One

The Evolution of Connectivity

The foundation of digital connectivity traces back to human desire for communication over distance. From smoke signals to telegraphs, communication has always been pivotal to societal development. The 20th century saw a revolution with electronic communication. Computers, initially large and isolated, became linked through emerging networks. The innovation of packet switching changed the paradigm allowing data to be split into packets traveling independent routes before reassembly. This technique made networks more reliable and efficient, forming the backbone of what became the internet.

In the late 1960s, ARPANET linked universities and research institutions, pioneering decentralized communication. Unlike telephone networks relying on fixed circuits, ARPANET dynamically routed packets. The introduction of Transmission Control Protocol and Internet Protocol (TCP/IP) standardized inter-computer communication enabling different networks to join into an internet. This interoperability was a cornerstone for the internet's growth.

The 1990s heralded the World Wide Web, introduced by Tim Berners-Lee, which transformed the internet into an accessible space for the public. Hypertext markup language (HTML), browsers, and hyperlinks made navigation intuitive. Businesses and governments recognized the web's potential, leading to widespread adoption. Email became commonplace, e-commerce grew, and digital services diversified rapidly. Mobile technologies accelerated connectivity's expansion. Smartphones combined communication, computing, and internet access in handheld devices, enabling users to stay connected everywhere. Mobile applications extended functionality beyond simple browsing, integrating payments, health monitoring, navigation, and social networking. These developments have changed user expectations, making constant connectivity essential.

Simultaneously, the Internet of Things connected everyday objects from refrigerators to vehicles. Sensors and actuators embedded in devices created intelligent environments that respond to user needs automatically. Smart cities emerged with connected infrastructure for energy management, transportation, and public safety. This integration fostered efficiency but also amplified complexity and security risks. Every connected device becomes a potential vulnerability in a vast ecosystem. Behind the scenes, cloud computing revolutionized how data and services are delivered. Instead of local storage and processing, the cloud provides on-demand resources across distributed data centers worldwide. Virtualization and containerization technologies enable efficient resource use, flexibility, and resilience. Businesses leverage the cloud for scalability, innovation, and collaboration. However, this dependence creates new attack surfaces and shifts trust towards service providers.

The physical layer of the internet is equally vital. Fiber optic cables span oceans, satellite constellations provide global coverage, and network hardware manages data flow. These infrastructures form a hidden web supporting digital life. Disruptions at this level can have widespread effects, as witnessed in cable cuts or undersea cable failures. The internet's robustness depends on constant maintenance, upgrades, and protection from physical and cyber threats.

The evolution of connectivity has outpaced regulatory frameworks and security practices. Businesses prioritize innovation and user experience often at the expense of security. Users adopt new devices and platforms rapidly, unaware of underlying risks. This gap between progress and protection leaves ecosystems exposed to exploitation. Threat actors exploit vulnerabilities in software, protocols, human behavior, and organizational weaknesses.

The immense scale of global connectivity creates systemic risks. A single flaw in a widely used software component or cloud service can compromise millions. The interconnected nature of networks means attacks can propagate quickly, affecting critical services and infrastructure. The COVID-19 pandemic underscored this dependence as remote work and digital services surged, exposing gaps in security preparedness.

Connectivity continues to expand with emerging technologies such as 5G, edge computing, and quantum communication. These innovations promise higher speeds, lower latency, and novel applications in augmented reality, autonomous systems, and AI integration. Yet each advance introduces new complexities and vulnerabilities. The digital ecosystem grows richer and more fragile simultaneously.

Understanding connectivity's evolution highlights that cybersecurity is not merely a technical challenge but a socio-technical one. The architecture of networks, devices, services, users, and policies form a complex adaptive system. Safeguarding this system requires holistic approaches that consider technology, human factors, economics, and governance. The future of connectivity depends on balancing innovation with security and trust.

The Illusion of Security

As connectivity grew, so did the need to protect digital assets. Early on, security measures were basic and reactive. Passwords, firewalls, and antivirus software served as primary defenses. These tools provided a sense of safety but often offered inadequate protection against evolving threats. The rapid expansion of the internet created new attack surfaces and opportunities for exploitation that security frameworks were unprepared for. Users and organizations frequently overestimated their security posture. Passwords were reused and weak. Firewalls were misconfigured or bypassed. Antivirus software relied on signature-based detection, insufficient against novel or polymorphic malware. The complexity of networks and devices made comprehensive security challenging. Many threats exploited human behavior rather than technological weaknesses, using social engineering, phishing, and manipulation.

Cybersecurity was often viewed as a technical issue isolated to IT teams. Business leaders treated it as a cost center or compliance checkbox. This mindset delayed investment in robust security programs and awareness training. Many organizations lacked incident response plans or threat intelligence capabilities. The result was frequent data breaches, ransomware attacks, and disruptions that could have been mitigated.

Attackers evolved from opportunistic hackers to sophisticated adversaries. Organized crime groups monetized cybercrime with ransomware-as-a-service, phishing campaigns, and identity theft. Nation-states engaged in espionage, sabotage, and influence operations. Insider threats increased, with disgruntled employees or negligent staff causing significant damage. The threat landscape became multifaceted and persistent. The illusion that technology alone could ensure security became dangerous. Attackers exploited zero-day vulnerabilities, supply chain weaknesses, and cloud misconfigurations. Software dependencies created cascading risks. IoT devices often lacked basic security features, exposing homes and industries. Mobile applications requested excessive permissions, collecting sensitive user data without clear controls. Users generally lacked cybersecurity awareness. Many failed to recognize phishing attempts or suspicious activity. Default security settings went unchanged. The convenience of “single sign-on” and automatic logins traded off with risk. Behavioral factors such as overconfidence, complacency, and distraction amplified vulnerabilities. Security is only as strong as the weakest link.

The cybersecurity industry gradually shifted to proactive defense and resilience. Concepts such as defense in depth, zero trust architectures, and continuous monitoring emerged. Threat intelligence sharing and coordinated responses became vital. Regulatory frameworks introduced requirements for breach notification, data protection, and cybersecurity governance. Yet adoption remains uneven across sectors and regions. The gap between perceived and actual security remains a significant challenge. Many individuals and organizations maintain a false sense of safety, underestimating threats or ignoring warning signs. The consequences of this illusion are severe, including financial loss, reputational damage, and compromised privacy. Public awareness campaigns and education are crucial but must be sustained and evolving. Cybersecurity is ultimately a shared responsibility. Technology vendors, service providers, organizations, governments, and users must collaborate. Security must be integrated into design, development, deployment, and operation of digital systems. Culture change is needed to embed security awareness and accountability at every level. Only through collective vigilance can the illusion be replaced by informed preparedness.

The Architecture of Digital Risk

Digital risk stems from the complexity and interconnectedness of modern technology ecosystems. No system exists in isolation.

Enterprises rely on cloud providers, third-party software, hardware manufacturers, and global supply chains. Each layer introduces dependencies and potential points of failure. The scale and heterogeneity of these systems amplify the difficulty of securing them. Cloud computing is a major factor in today's digital risk landscape. Cloud platforms centralize resources but create concentrated targets. Misconfigured storage buckets, insecure APIs, and insufficient access controls expose sensitive data. Trust shifts from local administrators to cloud providers, requiring rigorous governance and audits. Multi-cloud strategies complicate management further but can provide redundancy. The proliferation of IoT devices adds another dimension. These devices often run lightweight software with limited security features and infrequent updates. Many connect through wireless protocols susceptible to interception or spoofing. Their integration with operational technology creates risks for critical infrastructure, including energy, transportation, and healthcare sectors. Attacks on these systems can cause physical harm.

Mobile ecosystems bring risks through fragmented app stores, diverse operating systems, and wide user bases. Applications may request permissions beyond their needs, collect data without transparency, or harbor vulnerabilities. Mobile devices serve as gateways into corporate networks through bring-your-own-device policies. Securing mobile endpoints requires a combination of technical controls and user education. Artificial intelligence introduces both risks and opportunities. AI systems depend on data quality, model robustness, and interpretability. Adversarial attacks can manipulate inputs to produce incorrect outputs. Bias in training data leads to unfair or dangerous decisions. AI also powers advanced threat detection and response but demands expertise and vigilance to avoid new vulnerabilities.

Human factors remain a critical element of risk architecture. Social engineering attacks exploit cognitive biases, urgency, authority, and trust. Phishing, spear-phishing, and business email compromise continue to cause significant losses. Insider threats from negligence or malice require monitoring, clear policies, and ethical workplace cultures. Security awareness training is vital but must be regularly updated to remain effective.

Governance and compliance frameworks shape risk management practices. Regulations such as GDPR, HIPAA, and CCPA impose requirements on data protection and breach handling. Industry standards provide guidelines for controls and audits. However, inconsistent enforcement and varying legal regimes complicate global operations. Organizations must navigate a patchwork of obligations while striving for comprehensive security.

Incident response and recovery capabilities complete the risk architecture. No system is invulnerable. Preparing for breaches, detecting incidents promptly, containing damage, and restoring operations quickly minimize impact. Simulation exercises, clear communication channels, and cross-functional coordination improve resilience. Lessons learned feed back into improved defenses.

Understanding digital risk as an architectural challenge rather than isolated problems enables more effective strategies. Security must be designed holistically, considering technical, human, and organizational dimensions. Investment in talent, tools, processes, and culture is essential. Collaboration across sectors, public-private partnerships, and international cooperation strengthen collective defense.

The journey to secure connectivity is ongoing and dynamic. Threats will evolve as technology advances. Vigilance, adaptation, and innovation must be continuous. The architecture of digital risk demands not only protection but agility and foresight. Only then can the benefits of a hyper-connected world be realized without succumbing to its dangers.

Chapter Two

Emerging Threats in a Connected World

As the digital ecosystem expands in complexity and scope, new threats emerge with increasing frequency and sophistication. The evolving landscape of cyber threats reflects not only advances in technology but also shifts in geopolitical tensions, economic motivations, and social engineering tactics. Today's adversaries range from lone hackers seeking recognition to well-funded state-sponsored groups conducting espionage or sabotage. Understanding these emerging threats requires an examination of their nature, methods, and implications. Ransomware has become one of the most pervasive and damaging threats globally. This form of malware encrypts victims' data and demands payment for its release. Early ransomware attacks targeted individuals and small businesses, but over time attackers shifted focus toward larger organizations, critical infrastructure, and government entities. The rise of ransomware-as-a-service lowered barriers for cybercriminals, allowing less skilled operators to launch sophisticated attacks by renting malware infrastructure. The consequences are devastating, disrupting essential services, causing financial losses, and eroding public trust.

Supply chain attacks represent a new frontier of vulnerability. Rather than attacking a target directly, adversaries compromise a supplier, vendor, or software provider to gain access to multiple organizations simultaneously. This strategy exploits trust relationships and can evade traditional defenses focused on perimeter security. High-profile incidents have exposed widespread weaknesses in third-party risk management and highlighted the need for continuous monitoring and stringent vetting procedures. The interdependence of modern business ecosystems means a single compromised partner can create cascading damage.

Artificial intelligence and machine learning are double-edged swords in cybersecurity. On one hand, they empower defenders with predictive analytics, automated threat detection, and response capabilities. On the other hand, attackers employ AI to develop adaptive malware, automate phishing campaigns, and evade detection through polymorphic code. The arms race between attackers and defenders increasingly revolves around data quality, algorithmic transparency, and model robustness. AI also raises concerns about deepfake technology, which can fabricate realistic audio and video to deceive individuals and manipulate public opinion. The Internet of Things dramatically enlarges the attack surface. Many IoT devices operate with limited security features and receive infrequent updates. Their integration into critical infrastructure, healthcare, and consumer environments poses significant risks. Vulnerabilities in connected medical devices can endanger patient safety, while compromised industrial control systems can disrupt manufacturing and utilities. The scale and diversity of IoT devices challenge traditional security models and require innovative approaches to threat detection and mitigation.

Cloud security remains a significant concern as organizations migrate infrastructure and services to cloud providers. Misconfigurations, weak access controls, and inadequate monitoring expose sensitive data to unauthorized access. The shared responsibility model places some security burdens on customers, who often lack visibility into provider controls. Attackers exploit these gaps through credential theft, privilege escalation, and supply chain compromises affecting cloud environments. Securing multi-cloud architectures demands comprehensive governance, continuous assessment, and collaboration between providers and clients.

Emerging communication technologies like 5G introduce both opportunities and risks. The enhanced speed, reduced latency, and massive device connectivity enable transformative applications such as autonomous vehicles and smart cities. However, the distributed and software-defined nature of 5G networks creates new vulnerabilities. Network slicing, virtualization, and edge computing components require robust security frameworks. The rapid deployment of 5G without standardized security protocols increases exposure to attacks, making coordinated industry and governmental efforts critical.

Threat actors also leverage social engineering techniques with greater sophistication. Phishing campaigns are increasingly targeted, personalized, and convincing. Attackers exploit social media profiles, public data, and organizational hierarchies to craft believable messages. Business email compromise scams manipulate employees into authorizing fraudulent payments or revealing confidential information. Psychological manipulation remains one of the most effective tactics, bypassing technical controls by exploiting human trust and error.

Cryptocurrency and blockchain technologies have introduced novel challenges. While blockchain offers transparent and tamper-resistant ledgers, cryptocurrency transactions are often irreversible and pseudonymous, attracting illicit activity. Ransomware operators demand payments in cryptocurrency, complicating tracking and recovery efforts. Initial coin offerings and decentralized finance platforms have been used for scams and money laundering. Regulatory uncertainty and the evolving nature of these technologies require adaptive oversight to balance innovation with security.

The geopolitical landscape increasingly influences cyber threats. Nation-states engage in cyber espionage, intellectual property theft, disinformation campaigns, and attacks on critical infrastructure. Cyber warfare blurs traditional boundaries of conflict, with state actors operating covertly to advance strategic objectives. Attribution remains challenging, complicating international responses and deterrence. Global cooperation is essential to establish norms and reduce the risk of escalation.

In summary, the connected world faces a constantly shifting threat environment characterized by technological advances, evolving tactics, and diverse motivations. Defenders must remain vigilant, adaptive, and collaborative to counter these challenges. Understanding the emerging threats forms the foundation for effective cybersecurity strategies.

The Human Factor in Cybersecurity

Technology continues to evolve at a staggering pace, but the most consistent vulnerability in any system remains human behavior. Even the most advanced security infrastructure can be compromised by a single individual who clicks a malicious link, falls for a scam, or uses a weak password. Cybersecurity is not merely a technical field; it is deeply human. Understanding the psychology, habits, and decision-making patterns of individuals is essential to building resilient systems.

Human error is the root cause of a majority of security incidents. These errors are rarely the result of malice. More often, they stem from fatigue, distraction, insufficient training, or assumptions. Employees may reuse passwords across platforms, share credentials informally, or bypass security procedures for the sake of convenience. In high-pressure environments, speed is prioritized over scrutiny. Without a culture that reinforces secure behaviors, these practices become normalized. Social engineering exploits human psychology to manipulate individuals into compromising security. Attackers impersonate colleagues, pose as authority figures, or create a false sense of urgency to pressure targets into acting without verification. Phishing emails are no longer generic. They are tailored, persuasive, and often indistinguishable from legitimate communication. These attacks succeed not because of technical brilliance, but because they exploit trust, curiosity, fear, and routine. Insider threats present another dimension of human risk. Not all threats come from outside the organization. Disgruntled employees, contractors with access privileges, or even careless staff can cause immense damage. Some insiders deliberately steal data or sabotage systems, while others inadvertently expose sensitive information through poor practices. Managing insider threats requires a balance of monitoring, policy enforcement, and respect for privacy.

Training and awareness programs are the first line of defense against human error. However, many such programs are ineffective due to generic content, lack of engagement, or infrequent delivery. Cybersecurity training must be relevant, ongoing, and integrated into organizational culture. It should include simulated attacks, real-world examples, and clear reporting channels. Employees must understand that security is everyone's responsibility, not just the IT department's concern. Leadership plays a critical role in shaping cybersecurity culture. Executives must lead by example, invest in training, and support security initiatives. When leadership communicates the importance of security and models appropriate behaviors, employees are more likely to follow suit. Conversely, when leadership neglects security or prioritizes short-term goals over risk mitigation, the entire organization suffers.

Stress, fatigue, and overwork contribute significantly to security lapses. Cybersecurity requires attention, judgment, and discipline qualities that diminish under stress. Organizations must recognize that workforce well-being directly influences security posture. Adequate staffing, reasonable workloads, and mental health support are not just ethical imperatives; they are practical security measures.

Generational and cultural differences also impact cybersecurity behavior. Digital natives may be more comfortable with technology but also more likely to assume systems are secure by default. Older employees may be more cautious but less familiar with emerging threats. Cross-cultural teams bring valuable diversity but may also face challenges aligning on security norms and expectations. Tailored training and inclusive communication strategies help bridge these gaps.

The transition to remote and hybrid work has amplified the human factor. Home networks, personal devices, and relaxed environments blur the line between professional and personal activity. Employees may connect to unsecured Wi-Fi, store files on personal devices, or use unapproved applications. Monitoring and enforcing security policies becomes more difficult outside the controlled office environment. Organizations must adapt policies, tools, and training to this new reality without sacrificing flexibility and autonomy.

Ultimately, technology alone cannot solve human vulnerabilities. Firewalls cannot stop an employee from clicking a phishing link. Encryption cannot protect data if someone gives away the decryption key. Security must be intuitive, integrated, and supportive of human behavior rather than working against it. Building secure systems means building systems that people can use securely.

Strategies for Proactive Defense

The complexity and dynamism of modern cyber threats demand a shift from reactive to proactive defense. Waiting for incidents to occur before taking action is a strategy doomed to failure in a hyper-connected world. Proactive cybersecurity focuses on anticipating, preventing, and responding to threats before they escalate. It requires a combination of technological capability, strategic planning, and organizational discipline.

The foundation of proactive defense is visibility. You cannot protect what you cannot see. Organizations must have a clear, real-time understanding of their digital assets, including devices, applications, data flows, and user behaviors. Asset inventories should be accurate, comprehensive, and continuously updated. Endpoint detection and response solutions monitor for unusual activity and alert security teams to anomalies. Network traffic analysis, log aggregation, and threat hunting activities uncover hidden threats and vulnerabilities. Risk assessment is the next step. Not all assets are equally valuable or equally vulnerable. Organizations must prioritize their efforts based on potential impact and likelihood of attack. Business-critical systems, sensitive data, and key infrastructure require enhanced protection. This involves identifying single points of failure, evaluating supply chain dependencies, and considering both external and internal threat vectors.

Zero trust architecture is a core principle of proactive cybersecurity. It assumes that no user or device, even inside the network, should be trusted by default. Every request for access is verified, authenticated, and authorized based on dynamic context. Implementing zero trust requires granular access controls, multifactor authentication, micro-segmentation, and continuous monitoring. While challenging to implement fully, this model significantly reduces the attack surface and limits the spread of breaches.

Patch management is a critical yet often overlooked component of defense. Software vendors regularly release updates to address security flaws, but many organizations delay or neglect these updates, exposing themselves to known vulnerabilities. A disciplined patch management process includes testing updates in controlled environments, scheduling deployments, and verifying installation. Automation tools can help streamline this process across complex environments.

Employee training must be ongoing and scenario-based. Static training modules quickly become outdated in a fast-changing threat landscape. Simulated phishing campaigns, tabletop exercises, and interactive learning reinforce key concepts and prepare employees for real-world situations. Security awareness must be part of onboarding, performance evaluations, and organizational communication. Incident response planning transforms panic into action. Proactive organizations develop detailed response plans that define roles, responsibilities, communication channels, and recovery steps. Regular testing ensures these plans remain effective and familiar to all stakeholders. Response plans should include legal and regulatory considerations, customer notification procedures, and coordination with law enforcement when appropriate.

Backup and recovery strategies are vital defenses against ransomware and data loss. Backups should be encrypted, tested regularly, and stored in locations isolated from production systems. Recovery procedures must be documented and rehearsed. Organizations must know how quickly they can restore operations and what data they can afford to lose. Business continuity planning complements technical recovery by addressing operational and reputational impacts.

Threat intelligence enables informed decision-making. By analyzing global threat trends, tactics, and indicators of compromise, organizations can anticipate and prepare for likely attacks. Intelligence feeds may come from public sources, private vendors, or industry sharing groups. Integrating threat intelligence into security operations allows for dynamic response and contextual risk understanding.

Security information and event management systems provide centralized visibility and analysis. SIEM platforms collect logs and alerts from across the organization, correlating events to detect patterns and trigger response workflows. Machine learning capabilities enhance detection and reduce noise. SIEM integration with incident response tools enables rapid containment and forensics.

Governance and compliance structures ensure accountability and consistency. Proactive defense must be supported by policies, procedures, and leadership commitment. Security should be embedded into procurement, software development, and project planning. Audits, metrics, and continuous improvement drive maturity and resilience. A strong governance framework bridges the gap between strategy and execution.

Cyber insurance is an emerging component of risk management. While not a substitute for defense, insurance policies can help offset financial losses and facilitate recovery. Understanding policy coverage, exclusions, and requirements is essential. Insurers often require baseline security practices, encouraging better hygiene across the insured population. Proactive defense is not about eliminating all risk. That is impossible. It is about reducing the likelihood of incidents, minimizing their impact, and accelerating recovery. It is about resilience, not perfection. The organizations that thrive in the digital age will be those that treat cybersecurity as a continuous journey, not a destination.

Chapter Three

The Cybersecurity Lifecycle in Modern Infrastructure

In today's hyper-connected world cybersecurity is not a one-time investment or a singular task performed in response to a breach it is a continuous lifecycle that spans design implementation maintenance and decommissioning of every digital system. The lifecycle reflects a mindset that values proactive planning real-time vigilance adaptive defense and continuous improvement. Cybersecurity is not only about preventing attacks but also about preparing for them detecting them swiftly responding effectively and recovering with resilience. This lifecycle is deeply embedded into every modern infrastructure whether cloud-based mobile distributed or hybrid and understanding it is essential to protecting assets users and systems at scale.

The cybersecurity lifecycle begins at the earliest stage of system design. Security by design is a principle that integrates security considerations into the architecture of software hardware and infrastructure from the ground up. It involves identifying potential threats understanding how assets could be targeted modeling attacker behavior and building controls that mitigate those risks before the system is ever deployed. Threat modeling techniques such as STRIDE or PASTA help engineers think like attackers mapping out how a system could be exploited and ensuring that appropriate controls are embedded at each stage. Security cannot be added effectively as an afterthought. If the foundations are weak no amount of patching can provide long-term protection.

Once systems are deployed they enter an operational phase that demands active monitoring and threat detection. This includes tracking access logs analyzing traffic patterns scanning for vulnerabilities and observing behavioral anomalies. Monitoring tools such as Security Information and Event Management systems collect and correlate massive volumes of data to surface suspicious activities in real time. Threat intelligence feeds and behavioral analytics further enhance detection capabilities allowing teams to recognize zero-day threats unusual patterns or coordinated attacks before they escalate. This stage is about visibility context and speed. The sooner a threat is detected the smaller its potential impact. Detection is only the beginning. An effective response plan is critical and must be both strategic and tactical. This includes incident classification impact analysis root cause identification and coordinated mitigation steps. Well-defined incident response playbooks streamline decision-making during crises ensuring that communication is clear responsibilities are known and actions are immediate. Delays confusion or miscommunication can worsen the damage. Legal teams PR departments and executive leadership should all be included in response simulations so that the organization is not caught unprepared. Public disclosures regulatory obligations and customer communications must be handled with care and precision.

Following response the recovery stage restores normal operations while reinforcing future preparedness. Recovery goes beyond technical restoration. It encompasses restoring stakeholder trust rebuilding reputation and evaluating what went wrong. Backup systems are tested for integrity response actions are reviewed and systems may be redesigned to prevent recurrence. Recovery also involves learning. Every incident presents an opportunity to refine procedures improve defenses and update training. Organizations that approach incidents with transparency accountability and a focus on improvement emerge stronger and more resilient.

The final but often overlooked phase of the lifecycle is decommissioning. Systems data accounts and devices eventually reach end-of-life and must be retired securely. Improper decommissioning leaves traces that can be exploited by attackers including forgotten access credentials exposed configurations or unencrypted data. Secure disposal involves data sanitization revoking permissions and removing system access entirely. It also includes updating asset inventories and ensuring all third-party integrations are properly terminated. Failure at this stage can create long-term liabilities. Throughout the cybersecurity lifecycle continuous assessment and optimization are critical. Risks evolve new vulnerabilities emerge and threat actors adapt. Static defenses quickly become obsolete. Organizations must embrace continuous improvement driven by audits simulations performance metrics and threat intelligence. Security metrics should include mean time to detect mean time to respond false positive rates patching timelines and user awareness levels. Regular assessments reveal weaknesses in policy technology and personnel and guide strategic investments.

Automation plays a growing role in the lifecycle. Automated detection response and remediation accelerate reaction times reduce errors and scale defense across large environments. However automation must be guided by clear logic transparency and human oversight. Overreliance on automation without understanding the logic behind decisions can create blind spots. The combination of human judgment and machine precision is the hallmark of modern security operations. Cloud-based infrastructures require unique adaptations to the lifecycle. Shared responsibility models shift certain controls to the cloud provider while retaining others with the customer. Security teams must understand what they are accountable for and how provider tools integrate with their internal monitoring systems. Cloud environments are dynamic scalable and ephemeral. Traditional perimeter-based defenses are ineffective. Identity becomes the new perimeter and secure configuration access control encryption and continuous monitoring are essential. Mobile and edge computing environments also present distinct challenges. Devices may move between networks store sensitive data offline and operate with intermittent connectivity. Security policies must be adaptive context-aware and capable of enforcing controls at the endpoint. Mobile device management tools secure applications remote wipe capabilities and encrypted communications all play critical roles. Edge devices particularly those in industrial environments may operate for years with limited updates. Ensuring long-term integrity and secure firmware is crucial. The cybersecurity lifecycle is more than a technical framework. It reflects an organizational mindset that security is dynamic embedded and continuous. It is not a finish line it is a cycle that repeats with every update deployment and innovation. In a world where threats are constant the lifecycle becomes the heartbeat of digital resilience. Organizations that embed this lifecycle into their culture and operations will not only defend more effectively but will also adapt more quickly recover more completely and grow more confidently.

Governance Risk and Compliance in a Digital Era

Cybersecurity governance encompasses the frameworks leadership policies and accountability mechanisms that guide how security is managed across an organization. Risk represents the potential for harm resulting from threats exploiting vulnerabilities. Compliance refers to adhering to external regulations and internal policies. Together governance risk and compliance form the strategic backbone of an effective cybersecurity posture. In an era defined by digital transformation global interconnectivity and rising cyber threats these elements are more important than ever. Governance begins with leadership. Boards of directors and executive leadership must recognize cybersecurity as a business risk not just an IT issue. Cyber incidents affect revenue customer trust brand reputation and legal standing. Effective governance involves assigning clear roles and responsibilities defining risk appetite allocating budgets and overseeing performance. Leadership must ask critical questions about how risk is measured how incidents are handled and whether investments align with evolving threats.

Policies and procedures codify expectations and guide behavior. Acceptable use policies data classification guidelines incident response procedures and access control rules ensure consistency and accountability. Policies should be living documents updated regularly and communicated clearly. Too often policies are either ignored due to complexity or outdated due to evolving technology. Governance frameworks such as NIST CSF ISO 27001 and COBIT provide structured approaches for aligning cybersecurity with business goals. Risk management involves identifying assessing prioritizing and mitigating potential threats. This process includes asset discovery threat modeling vulnerability assessment impact analysis and likelihood estimation. Risk assessments should be tailored to the organization's industry regulatory landscape and operational profile. They should consider insider threats physical security third-party dependencies and emerging technologies. Risks must be translated into terms executives understand such as financial loss reputational damage legal exposure and operational downtime.

Third-party risk is one of the most pressing challenges in modern cybersecurity. Organizations rely on vendors partners cloud providers and contractors who may introduce vulnerabilities. A breach in one vendor can expose hundreds of downstream clients. Governance must include processes for vetting vendors conducting security assessments establishing contractual requirements and monitoring ongoing compliance. Supply chain attacks have made it clear that trust must be earned and verified not assumed. Compliance adds another layer of complexity. Different industries and jurisdictions impose different rules regarding data protection breach notification privacy and cybersecurity practices. Regulations such as GDPR HIPAA PCI-DSS and CCPA carry legal penalties for noncompliance. Compliance is not merely about avoiding fines. It is about aligning practices with societal expectations protecting consumer rights and demonstrating responsibility. Compliance requires documentation evidence internal audits and independent assessments. Audits and metrics validate governance effectiveness. Internal and external audits evaluate whether controls are implemented operating as intended and aligned with policies. Metrics such as patch compliance user training rates incident response times and risk acceptance levels provide insight into performance. Dashboards and scorecards help communicate progress to stakeholders and guide strategic decisions. Governance is not static. It evolves through feedback learning and adaptation.

Security awareness and training are core governance functions. Policies mean little if employees do not understand them or apply them. Awareness programs should cover phishing prevention password hygiene social engineering reporting procedures and role-based risks. They must be reinforced regularly adapted to current threats and evaluated for effectiveness. Governance ensures that training is prioritized resourced and aligned with organizational culture.

Crisis management and communication planning are essential components of governance. In the event of a breach organizations must act decisively and transparently. Communication strategies should be predefined including notifications to regulators customers partners and the public. Mishandling a breach can compound the damage. Effective governance includes rehearsing breach scenarios maintaining communication templates and empowering incident response leaders. Governance also supports ethical considerations. Surveillance data collection algorithmic decision-making and automated enforcement all raise ethical questions. Governance ensures that cybersecurity practices respect privacy civil liberties and human rights. It guides decision-making around proportionality necessity and fairness. Ethical governance builds trust with employees customers and society at large. In a digital era where cyber threats intersect with every aspect of business governance risk and compliance are not optional add-ons. They are foundational enablers of security resilience and trust. Organizations that lead with governance anticipate threats adapt with agility and operate with confidence. Those that neglect it risk not only breaches but also erosion of legitimacy and long-term viability.

Cyber Resilience Beyond Technology

Cyber resilience is the ability of an organization to continue operating during and after a cyber incident by absorbing shocks adapting to disruption and accelerating recovery. Unlike traditional security which focuses on prevention resilience acknowledges that some incidents are inevitable. The focus shifts from perfect defense to sustained performance and rapid adaptation. Resilience is about continuity not just protection. It goes beyond technology to include people processes culture leadership and learning.

The foundation of cyber resilience is a clear understanding of critical functions. Organizations must identify which processes systems and data are essential to mission continuity. This prioritization informs backup strategies failover architectures incident response plans and communication protocols. Not all systems require the same level of protection. By focusing resources where they matter most organizations can build targeted and effective resilience. Scenario planning and tabletop exercises prepare teams for real-world events. These exercises simulate ransomware attacks insider threats supply chain compromises and other plausible incidents. They test decision-making coordination escalation paths and communication strategies. Teams discover gaps in plans clarify roles and build confidence. Regular exercises embed resilience into culture making response actions instinctive and coordinated rather than improvised.

Leadership plays a pivotal role in establishing cyber resilience beyond the confines of technology. Executives and board members must understand cyber risk not only as an IT issue but as a business continuity and strategic concern. Leaders who prioritize cybersecurity in budgeting planning and culture send a clear message throughout the organization. They set the tone for vigilance responsible data stewardship and accountability. Without leadership buy-in even the most advanced security technologies fail to be effectively utilized. Leaders must also practice scenario thinking simulating worst-case cyber incidents and aligning response plans to those realities. They must champion resilience as an enterprise-wide objective not simply an IT function.

Culture is another invisible yet critical component of cyber resilience. A resilient organization fosters a security-aware culture where employees at all levels recognize the importance of safe practices report suspicious activities and follow defined protocols even under pressure. Cultural resilience means people understand that cybersecurity is a shared responsibility not the domain of specialists alone. This cultural mindset is cultivated through consistent messaging training recognition and empowerment. When individuals feel they are part of the defense not just subjects of enforcement they engage more meaningfully. Trust transparency and open communication form the bedrock of this culture.

Processes and planning are the structural pillars of cyber resilience beyond tools and platforms. This includes maintaining up-to-date incident response playbooks, cross-functional crisis management teams, clearly defined communication protocols and robust recovery procedures. Effective organizations rehearse these plans regularly through tabletop exercises red teaming and live simulations. These practices identify hidden vulnerabilities improve coordination and reduce panic during real incidents. Business continuity planning must account for both the technological and operational sides of disruption ensuring not only that systems come back online but also that essential services and workflows are re-established without confusion or delay.

The human dimension also encompasses emotional and psychological resilience. Cyber incidents create stress confusion fear and even guilt especially for those who may feel responsible. A resilient organization prepares its people emotionally. This includes building adaptive capacity in teams encouraging psychological safety offering post-incident support and fostering a non-blame environment. Resilience in this context is about keeping morale intact managing anxiety and sustaining performance under pressure. Training programs must include crisis psychology awareness stress management techniques and role clarity in emergencies.

External relationships and social infrastructure are also vital to cyber resilience. No organization exists in isolation. Resilience depends on the strength of external partnerships industry collaboration and public-private coordination. Shared threat intelligence frameworks regulatory support and inter-organizational trust enhance resilience at a systemic level. When incidents occur organizations must be able to reach out to law enforcement incident response vendors regulators and peers to share information and mobilize joint action. Community trust and reputation built over time through honest communication and responsible behavior help contain reputational fallout when crises occur.

Legal and regulatory awareness further underpins non-technical aspects of resilience. Organizations must be ready to navigate legal obligations such as breach disclosure compliance timelines and communication with affected stakeholders. Legal teams should work closely with cybersecurity units to ensure that response plans align with jurisdictional requirements. This readiness prevents delays missteps and liability in the critical hours following an attack. The learning loop is perhaps the most overlooked yet defining element of long-term cyber resilience. Organizations that do not learn from breaches remain fragile. Those that embed learning into their operating model grow stronger. Post-incident reviews root cause analyses near-miss investigations and lessons-learned sessions must be conducted with rigor and transparency. Findings must translate into tangible improvements in policy configuration training and culture. Organizational memory must preserve this knowledge so that experience is not lost through turnover or complacency.

Resilience must also be supported by investment in people development. The creation of multidisciplinary teams that include not only security experts but also risk managers legal advisors communicators and operations leaders ensures holistic planning and response. Talent development programs succession planning and knowledge transfer initiatives contribute to institutional memory and adaptability. Cybersecurity is a field defined by rapid change. Continuous learning and flexibility must be woven into the DNA of the organization.

In the broader societal context cyber resilience reflects the robustness of national infrastructure educational systems digital literacy and public awareness. Societies that promote digital citizenship media literacy and critical thinking are more resistant to manipulation fraud and disinformation. Citizens must understand how to protect themselves from scams how to identify credible information and how to report suspicious activity. Government programs and community outreach strengthen societal defenses. Resilience in this context means that democracy commerce education and daily life can continue despite the pervasive risk of cyber disruption.

Leadership plays a central role in resilience. During crises executives must lead with clarity transparency and resolve. They must make decisions with limited information under time pressure and public scrutiny. Resilient leaders prepare by understanding technical issues building trusted teams establishing clear authority and rehearsing response scenarios. Communication must be honest timely and empathetic to maintain trust with employees customers and stakeholders. Culture amplifies or undermines resilience. In resilient cultures employees report issues without fear share knowledge collaborate across silos and prioritize mission over blame. Psychological safety encourages disclosure of mistakes lessons learned and continuous improvement. Organizations that stigmatize failure or punish transparency create hidden risks. Culture is shaped by leaders reinforced by policies and sustained through daily behavior. Redundancy and diversity reduce fragility. Redundant systems data backups communication channels and power sources provide alternatives when one path fails. Diversity in suppliers technologies and processes prevents single points of failure. Overcentralization creates brittleness. Decentralization increases adaptability. Resilient architectures assume failure and design around it.

Resilience includes external coordination. Cyber incidents often involve multiple parties including vendors regulators customers and law enforcement. Predefined contact lists information sharing protocols and mutual aid agreements enable rapid coordination. Membership in information sharing and analysis centers industry groups and public-private partnerships enhances situational awareness and response capacity. Post-incident reviews transform setbacks into progress. Every incident provides lessons about vulnerabilities assumptions decisions and behavior. Structured after-action reviews identify what worked what failed and what must change. Resilience grows through reflection adaptation and institutional memory. Organizations that fail to learn repeat mistakes. Those that do improve continuously.

Measurement enables improvement. Resilience metrics include recovery time objectives mean time to recovery incident containment time user impact levels and customer satisfaction. Surveys interviews and behavioral observations complement technical indicators. Dashboards communicate progress and support investment decisions. Metrics must be aligned with strategic goals not just technical performance. Ultimately cyber resilience reflects organizational maturity. It is not a checklist but a mindset. It embraces uncertainty complexity and disruption as inevitable. It prepares for them with humility discipline and courage. Resilience transforms cybersecurity from a defensive posture into a competitive advantage. In a world where threats are constant and change is rapid resilience is not just a shield. It is the core of sustainable digital success.

Chapter Four

The Economic Impact of Cyber Insecurity

The modern economy is intricately dependent on digital infrastructure. Every sector from finance to healthcare from transportation to education from manufacturing to entertainment relies on interconnected systems networks and platforms. With this dependence comes vulnerability and with vulnerability comes cost. The economic impact of cyber insecurity is vast multifaceted and steadily increasing. It includes direct financial losses operational disruptions reputational damage regulatory penalties diminished investor confidence and lost business opportunities. Understanding this impact is essential for governments enterprises investors and citizens to grasp the urgency of cybersecurity investments. Cybercrime now constitutes a multi-trillion-dollar global shadow economy. According to various international estimates cyberattacks cost the world economy more than six trillion dollars annually a figure projected to grow in the coming years. This includes ransomware payments business email compromise fraud intellectual property theft and data breaches. Yet this figure only scratches the surface. The hidden costs of cyber incidents including productivity loss opportunity cost and customer attrition often dwarf the immediate damages.

Direct losses are the most visible. These include stolen funds ransom payments repair costs data recovery legal fees and forensic investigations. When attackers gain access to financial systems they can siphon funds initiate fraudulent transactions or manipulate accounting records. In ransomware attacks victims may be forced to pay substantial sums often in cryptocurrency to regain access to encrypted data. Even when backups are available restoration costs and delays can be enormous. In some cases operational downtime costs millions per hour especially in industries like aviation logistics or manufacturing. Reputational damage represents a more insidious and long-lasting cost. When customers learn that their personal information has been compromised trust is eroded. Even loyal clients may choose to do business elsewhere fearing a lack of protection. Publicly traded companies often experience stock price declines following data breaches. Investor confidence can be shaken regulatory scrutiny can intensify and competitors may capitalize on the moment of weakness. Reputation is difficult to quantify but its loss can cripple a brand.

Regulatory fines and legal settlements add another layer of financial exposure. Governments around the world have enacted stringent data protection laws including the General Data Protection Regulation in Europe the California Consumer Privacy Act and sector-specific mandates like HIPAA in healthcare. Failure to comply with these regulations or failure to notify authorities and users promptly after a breach can result in substantial fines. Class action lawsuits may follow especially if negligence can be demonstrated. Legal liabilities extend beyond the breach itself into how the organization prepared responded and communicated. Insurance is increasingly used to manage cyber risk but it too has economic implications. Premiums for cyber insurance have surged in response to rising incident frequency and severity. Coverage exclusions have expanded policies have become more complex and insurers demand rigorous risk assessments before underwriting. Organizations may rely on insurance as a financial backstop but must still invest heavily in controls to meet policy requirements. Furthermore insurance cannot replace trust nor can it eliminate operational disruption.

Small and medium-sized businesses are disproportionately affected by cyberattacks. They often lack the resources expertise or infrastructure to defend themselves effectively. A single breach can lead to bankruptcy. These organizations are attractive targets because of perceived vulnerability. Even if not directly targeted they may be affected as part of broader supply chain attacks. The economic impact extends beyond the organization to employees suppliers customers and the communities that depend on them. The macroeconomic implications of cyber insecurity are profound. National economies are increasingly exposed to systemic cyber risks. An attack on financial infrastructure energy grids transportation systems or healthcare institutions can cause widespread disruption beyond individual firms. These incidents challenge economic stability reduce investor confidence and weaken national resilience. Governments must now factor cybersecurity into economic planning trade policy national security strategy and critical infrastructure protection.

Innovation suffers when insecurity prevails. Organizations may hesitate to adopt digital technologies if risks appear too great. Startups may struggle to gain traction if customers are wary of untested systems. Investments in digital transformation may stall when security concerns dominate. Conversely companies that lead in cybersecurity often gain competitive advantage. They attract customers partners and investors by demonstrating responsible stewardship of data and systems. The labor market is also shaped by cyber insecurity. Demand for cybersecurity professionals far outpaces supply leading to talent shortages increased salaries and intense competition. Organizations must invest in workforce development training and recruitment or risk falling behind. Cyber incidents may also affect employment directly as businesses reduce headcount to offset losses or as automation replaces compromised processes. A resilient workforce is critical to economic resilience.

At the global level cyber insecurity has become a factor in international competitiveness. Nations with strong cybersecurity ecosystems attract investment foster innovation and protect their citizens. Those that fail to secure their digital economies risk stagnation or decline. Cybersecurity is now a pillar of economic development not merely a technical function. It influences trade negotiations foreign investment defense alliances and diplomatic relations. Ultimately the economic impact of cyber insecurity cannot be overstated. It affects every level of the economy from individual consumers to multinational corporations from local businesses to global supply chains from national GDP to international relations. Addressing this challenge requires sustained investment in prevention detection response recovery and governance. The cost of insecurity is not just financial it is strategic cultural and existential. Cybersecurity is no longer optional it is foundational to economic prosperity.

Digital Trust and the Ethics of Protection

In the digital era trust is currency. Users entrust organizations with their personal data behaviors identities preferences and transactions often without fully understanding the scope or implications. Digital trust refers to the confidence users place in systems platforms and institutions to act responsibly securely and ethically. It is built slowly through transparency consistency and accountability but can be lost instantly through breach negligence or deception. As cybersecurity becomes more central to life online the ethical dimensions of protection rise to the forefront. The ethical obligation to protect users extends beyond technical competence. It includes respecting privacy ensuring fairness maintaining transparency and upholding dignity. Organizations collect analyze and share enormous volumes of personal data often using it to make automated decisions about employment credit healthcare and more. When security fails users bear the consequences. They may suffer identity theft financial loss reputational harm or emotional distress. The ethical principle of non-maleficence do no harm applies directly to cybersecurity practices.

Privacy is a cornerstone of digital trust. Ethical cybersecurity defends not just data but the rights of individuals to control how their information is used. This means minimizing data collection using data only for stated purposes ensuring informed consent and enabling access correction and deletion. It also means protecting against surveillance overreach whether by corporations governments or malicious actors. Privacy by design and privacy by default are ethical design principles that reinforce trust from the start.

Transparency is essential to trust. Users have the right to know what data is collected how it is used who has access and what protections are in place. They also have the right to be informed promptly in the event of a breach. Concealing incidents erodes trust. Ethical organizations communicate openly admit mistakes and take responsibility. They do not use complexity or ambiguity to obscure reality. Clear privacy policies accessible language and honest reporting are foundational. Inclusion and fairness must guide cybersecurity practices. Systems must work for everyone regardless of age race disability income or geography. Biometric systems facial recognition and behavioral analytics can exhibit bias leading to exclusion or discrimination. Ethical protection requires representative data inclusive design diverse teams and ongoing validation. It also means ensuring that marginalized groups are not disproportionately targeted or surveilled. Digital equity is an ethical imperative.

Security decisions have moral consequences. For example end-to-end encryption protects user privacy but can hinder law enforcement. Backdoors may aid investigation but weaken global security. Balancing competing rights and interests is complex. Ethical frameworks help navigate these tensions. They provide principles such as necessity proportionality transparency and accountability. Ethics boards multidisciplinary reviews and public engagement can guide responsible decision-making. The ethics of cybersecurity extend to artificial intelligence. AI systems can be used to detect threats personalize responses and automate defense. But they can also be used to manipulate deceive or exploit. Deepfakes misinformation social engineering and algorithmic bias pose ethical challenges. Developers must ensure that AI systems are explainable auditable fair and aligned with human values. Security must be embedded into the AI lifecycle from data curation to model deployment. Children and vulnerable populations require special protection. Minors may not understand consent digital risks or long-term consequences. Elderly users may fall victim to scams. Individuals with disabilities may face barriers to understanding or interacting with security systems. Ethical cybersecurity includes accessible interfaces protective defaults clear guidance and supportive communities. It also means developing policies that reflect social responsibilities not just technical feasibility. Supply chain ethics also matter. Organizations must ensure that their partners vendors and suppliers uphold security standards and ethical principles. This includes labor practices environmental sustainability and data governance. A breach in the supply chain is not just a technical failure it can be a moral one. Ethical procurement policies audits and due diligence processes help ensure alignment and integrity.

The ethical responsibilities of cybersecurity professionals must also be addressed. They hold privileged access to systems knowledge and capabilities. Codes of conduct licensing requirements ethical training and professional accountability mechanisms reinforce standards. The cybersecurity community must uphold integrity honesty and respect for rights. Whistleblower protections and ethical escalation paths support internal accountability. Digital trust is fragile. It cannot be bought legislated or outsourced. It must be earned through behavior. Ethics is not a constraint on cybersecurity it is its foundation. Security that ignores ethics may achieve short-term goals but ultimately fails to inspire confidence or foster sustainable progress. In a connected world protection must be ethical to be effective. The future of cybersecurity depends on the alignment of technical excellence and moral clarity.

Digital trust is not merely a byproduct of technological competence. It is a deliberate construct built through consistent behavior transparent governance ethical responsibility and the capacity to protect and respect users in a connected world. In an era where data drives decisions and identity is increasingly defined through digital footprints trust becomes the currency of interaction. Without trust the digital economy falters online relationships dissolve and the very infrastructure that supports innovation begins to collapse under the weight of suspicion and misuse. At its core digital trust demands not only technical excellence but a deep ethical commitment to fairness accountability privacy and security.

Trust must be earned not presumed. It grows from experiences where users believe their rights are honored their information is protected and their autonomy is respected. Organizations that misuse data fail to secure systems or obscure their practices rapidly erode trust. Users are acutely aware of breaches manipulations and dishonest communication. A single breach can wipe out years of trust built through engagement and brand loyalty. Therefore cultivating digital trust requires intentional ethical design from the foundation upward.

Ethical protection is the discipline of safeguarding not only data but dignity. It considers how technologies affect people's lives values and opportunities. Protection is not merely about stopping threats. It is about actively preventing harm anticipating misuse and fostering environments where people can thrive without fear of manipulation exploitation or surveillance. This dimension of protection requires foresight moral clarity and a willingness to make decisions that prioritize the well-being of users even when those choices may not maximize short-term profit.

Transparency lies at the heart of ethical digital trust. Users must be informed about how their data is collected used stored and shared. Clarity must replace complexity. Legal jargon hidden terms and obfuscating interfaces diminish trust. Ethical organizations embrace openness not because regulation demands it but because respect requires it. They inform users in ways that empower understanding and consent not passive compliance. They create interfaces that reinforce user control offering real choices and respecting decisions.

Consent must be meaningful not manipulated. It must be given freely with full knowledge of consequences and retained as a living agreement. Systems that assume consent through inactivity or that conceal critical options under dark patterns betray ethical design. The ethics of protection call for reframing consent as an ongoing conversation not a one-time checkbox. Users should be able to revisit choices withdraw permissions and understand the impact of their participation across time.

Accountability is the structural backbone of digital trust. Ethical protection fails when power lacks consequences. Organizations must be held to account for misuse of data for inadequate security and for enabling harmful outcomes through digital services. This accountability must be internal through governance and external through regulatory oversight civil society and public scrutiny. Mechanisms such as algorithmic audits privacy impact assessments and redress systems must be in place and accessible. Trust cannot flourish in systems that permit impunity or evade responsibility.

Inclusion is another pillar of ethical protection. Technologies must be designed with equity in mind ensuring that they serve all users fairly across lines of race gender ability and socioeconomic background. Bias in algorithms inaccessible interfaces and exclusionary practices undermine trust and perpetuate digital injustice. Ethical organizations proactively identify disparities address systemic disadvantages and design for the most vulnerable. Protection is not complete until it includes everyone.

Security must also be framed as a human right not a technical feature. It must be universally provided not selectively applied. People should not have to pay extra or possess specialized knowledge to be safe online. Cybersecurity should be built into devices platforms and services from inception. Ethical protection means designing systems where the default is secure where failure does not mean exposure and where updates repairs and assistance are available without discrimination.

Trust requires stewardship. Data should not be treated as property to be exploited but as responsibility to be guarded. The collection of personal information imposes a duty of care. This duty includes minimizing data collection limiting retention securing access and ensuring that any use aligns with the original intent and expectations of the user. Repurposing data without consent or trading it without transparency violates the ethics of protection and weakens the bonds of trust.

The ethics of protection also require resistance to surveillance excess. While monitoring may be justified for safety security or functionality it must be bounded by necessity proportionality and due process. Systems must avoid turning every user interaction into a point of observation. Excessive surveillance creates chilling effects distorts behavior and harms psychological well-being. It breeds fear not trust. Ethical organizations balance the need for insight with the right to anonymity autonomy and respect.

Digital trust also requires that systems resist manipulation. Techniques designed to addict deceive or coerce undermine agency. Whether through addictive design algorithms that prioritize outrage or nudges that exploit cognitive biases manipulative practices corrode ethical integrity. Protecting users includes shielding them from environments that hijack attention degrade self-control or feed harmful behaviors. Designing for well-being rather than engagement metrics is essential to an ethical digital ecosystem.

In global contexts ethical protection takes on additional complexity. Norms around privacy expression and autonomy vary across cultures and legal systems. Global platforms must navigate these differences with sensitivity yet uphold a universal standard of dignity and human rights. They must avoid becoming tools of oppression by resisting misuse by authoritarian regimes and ensuring that core protections travel with the user regardless of jurisdiction. Cross-border data flows must be governed by principles not just efficiency.

Education empowers trust. Users who understand digital systems can better exercise rights and avoid risks. Ethical protection includes a commitment to digital literacy not as a marketing strategy but as a public good. Empowered users can ask better questions make informed choices and demand better practices. Education must reach children elders marginalized communities and all who are at heightened risk of harm online. Ethical organizations invest in user education because they value agency not because they fear backlash.

Trust is also shaped by the response to harm. Mistakes and breaches will occur. What matters is how organizations respond. Swift transparent action support for affected users honest reflection and structural correction demonstrate integrity. Attempts to hide minimize or deflect blame destroy trust. Ethical protection is not about being perfect but about being accountable when things go wrong. Finally ethical protection must be future-focused. Decisions made today will shape digital trust for generations. The design of emerging technologies such as artificial intelligence brain-computer interfaces and immersive realities must embed ethical foresight from the beginning. Governance frameworks must evolve alongside innovation to protect against new harms while supporting discovery and progress. Future trust depends on the courage to question convenience to slow down when needed and to prioritize people over profit in the face of uncertain consequences. In conclusion digital trust and the ethics of protection demand more than compliance. They require conviction. They are built not through claims but through actions that align power with purpose. As the digital world becomes ever more enmeshed with daily life the responsibility to protect must deepen. Ethical protection is the promise that people can move through the digital world with confidence not fear. That they can build, create, connect, and belong without exploitation. It is a promise worth keeping. It is the only foundation upon which true digital trust can stand.

Global Collaboration in Cyber Defense

Cyber threats do not respect borders. Malware can originate in one country attack infrastructure in another and impact users on every continent within minutes. Threat actors operate across jurisdictions using encrypted communication global platforms and decentralized currencies. Cyberattacks may target governments corporations individuals or entire societies. Given the transnational nature of these challenges global collaboration is not just beneficial it is essential. Cyber defense requires a unified response that transcends politics competition and geography. International norms are the foundation of collaborative security. Just as international law governs conflict trade and diplomacy emerging norms must guide behavior in cyberspace. These include prohibiting attacks on critical infrastructure respecting sovereignty protecting civilian systems and avoiding indiscriminate malware deployment. Norms are developed through dialogue diplomacy and consensus. The United Nations the G7 the G20 and regional alliances all play roles in shaping these frameworks. While enforcement is difficult agreement on principles builds trust and reduces escalation. Information sharing is vital to rapid defense. Threat intelligence must flow across borders sectors and institutions. This includes indicators of compromise tactics techniques and procedures incident reports vulnerability disclosures and defensive strategies. Organizations like Computer Emergency Response Teams Information Sharing and Analysis Centers and global alliances facilitate this exchange. Public-private partnerships are particularly effective combining government resources with private sector agility. Joint exercises and simulations strengthen coordination. Cyber war games cross-border drills and multinational training programs help align procedures clarify responsibilities and build relationships. They prepare teams to respond to incidents involving multiple countries or sectors. They also reveal gaps in readiness legal barriers and cultural misunderstandings. Practicing collaboration under pressure enhances real-world response capabilities.

Capacity building ensures that all nations can participate in collective defense. Many countries lack the infrastructure expertise or institutions to defend against sophisticated attacks. International support includes funding technical assistance training and institution building. Development agencies nonprofits and multilateral banks can support cyber capacity alongside traditional aid. Digital resilience is part of national development and global stability.Diplomatic channels manage cyber conflicts. When a nation suspects another of cyber aggression dialogue is essential. Attribution is difficult miscalculation is dangerous and retaliation may escalate. Cyber diplomacy includes hotlines trust-building measures incident notification protocols and mutual assistance agreements. It also involves cooperation on criminal investigations extradition treaties and law enforcement training. Cybercrime requires global law enforcement coordination. Agencies like Interpol Europol and the FBI collaborate across jurisdictions. They share intelligence pursue fugitives dismantle infrastructure and coordinate arrests. Cybercrime units must navigate legal differences evidence standards language barriers and political sensitivities. Mutual legal assistance treaties and international conventions support these efforts. Research collaboration drives innovation. Academics researchers and technologists across the globe must work together to develop new defenses understand threats and shape policy. Conferences journals working groups and open source projects enable knowledge exchange. Diversity in thought methodology and perspective enhances innovation. Cybersecurity is a global science and global community.

Standardization promotes interoperability. International standards for encryption authentication device security and software development ensure compatibility and baseline protection. Organizations like the International Organization for Standardization the Internet Engineering Task Force and industry consortia create and maintain these standards. Adoption varies but convergence improves security at scale. Cybersecurity diplomacy includes values. Collaboration must reflect and reinforce human rights open internet principles freedom of expression and democratic norms. Authoritarian regimes may misuse cybersecurity to suppress dissent censor information or control populations. International engagement must balance cooperation with principled advocacy. Security cannot be separated from values.

Global collaboration is challenging. Sovereignty competition mistrust and legal differences complicate alignment. But isolation is not an option. In a connected world security is collective. When one nation or sector is vulnerable others are affected. Collaboration is not just about information or tools it is about relationships values and vision. The path forward requires courage commitment and creativity.

Chapter Five

Cybersecurity in Critical Infrastructure Systems

Critical infrastructure systems form the backbone of national security economic stability and public safety. These systems encompass energy grids water supply chains healthcare services transportation networks communication frameworks and financial operations. Any disruption in these sectors due to a cyber incident can trigger cascading consequences far beyond the immediate target. As digital transformation continues to modernize operational technology and integrate industrial control systems into broader networks the cybersecurity of critical infrastructure has evolved from a technical concern into a matter of national resilience. Historically many critical infrastructure components operated in isolated environments known as air-gapped systems that were not connected to the internet. While this separation once offered inherent security the modern push for operational efficiency remote management and real-time data analytics has eroded these boundaries. Supervisory Control and Data Acquisition systems programmable logic controllers and other operational technologies are now often networked enabling faster decision-making but also expanding the attack surface.

Nation-state actors often target critical infrastructure to achieve strategic objectives without engaging in open conflict. Cyberattacks against power grids oil pipelines water treatment facilities and transportation hubs serve as a form of digital warfare capable of disrupting lives economies and public confidence. High-profile incidents have revealed the fragility of these systems when targeted by well-resourced adversaries. These attacks are not speculative they are active components of modern geopolitical tension.

The integration of legacy systems into digital networks presents a significant challenge. Many industrial control systems were designed decades ago with reliability and uptime as the primary goals not cybersecurity. These systems often lack encryption authentication or update mechanisms and cannot easily be replaced due to cost regulatory constraints or operational dependencies. As a result defenders must protect vulnerable legacy components with modern tools while ensuring uninterrupted service. Risk assessments in critical infrastructure must be both sector-specific and function-oriented. A cyber incident in a hospital affects human life directly a disruption in air traffic control can halt an entire economy a breach in water purification systems can create widespread public health crises. Each sector has unique vulnerabilities dependencies and consequences. Therefore cyber risk management must be tailored to the specific physical and digital realities of the systems involved.

Collaboration between public and private sectors is essential. In many countries critical infrastructure is owned and operated by private entities while national security responsibilities reside with government agencies. This interdependence necessitates trust information sharing coordinated response planning and joint training. Sector-specific Information Sharing and Analysis Centers and national cyber emergency response teams facilitate these relationships and disseminate timely intelligence. Incident response in critical infrastructure demands real-time visibility and rapid containment. Traditional IT playbooks are insufficient. Operational continuity cannot be sacrificed for security remediation without severe consequences. Therefore defenders must design layered defenses segmented networks safety fallbacks and robust logging mechanisms. They must also prepare for manual overrides and analog redundancies in case digital systems fail or are compromised. Simulation and training exercises are invaluable. Tabletop scenarios live simulations and red team engagements help identify vulnerabilities evaluate response readiness and build cross-sector coordination. These exercises must involve both technical and executive leadership ensuring that business continuity decisions are informed by real-world dynamics. Clear communication chains defined authorities and rehearsed protocols reduce chaos during actual incidents. Supply chain security is a growing concern. Critical infrastructure relies on third-party components software and maintenance services that may be compromised or manipulated. A single vulnerability introduced by a subcontractor can affect thousands of systems. Rigorous vetting secure procurement requirements and end-to-end visibility are necessary to maintain integrity. Software bill of materials requirements and hardware provenance tracking are emerging practices in this space.Resilience is paramount. Not every attack can be prevented but damage can be minimized through architectural redundancy incident rehearsals backup power systems and decentralized control. Resilience includes not just restoring service but maintaining public trust mitigating secondary effects and preventing recurrence. Effective crisis communication plays a critical role. Transparency credibility and empathy help sustain public confidence even in the face of disruption.

Regulatory frameworks are evolving. Governments around the world are introducing cybersecurity requirements for critical infrastructure operators including mandatory reporting response standards and technical controls. Compliance is no longer optional. Operators must embed security into operations risk management strategy and procurement practices. Failure to comply not only exposes systems to attack but also invites regulatory penalties and reputational damage. Cybersecurity in critical infrastructure is not just a defense it is an enabler of national continuity. It protects the systems that keep lights on water flowing hospitals operational planes flying and economies functioning. In an era of increasing threats and interconnected risks the security of these systems must be treated with the same seriousness and urgency as physical defense. Their protection is not only a matter of technology it is a matter of survival.

Securing the Future of Financial Technology

The financial sector is undergoing a radical transformation driven by digital innovation decentralized technologies artificial intelligence and mobile platforms. Financial technology or fintech has redefined how money is saved moved invested and accessed. While this innovation brings convenience inclusion and efficiency it also introduces complex cybersecurity challenges. The integrity confidentiality and availability of financial systems are essential to societal function. A failure in trust or security can ripple across markets economies and lives. Fintech spans a vast landscape including online banking peer-to-peer payment systems digital wallets cryptocurrency exchanges investment platforms and algorithmic trading. Each of these technologies relies on digital infrastructure to operate at scale. The digitization of money has outpaced the security protocols governing it creating opportunities for fraud theft disruption and manipulation. Authentication and identity management are central to fintech security. Weak password policies reliance on SMS verification and lack of multi-factor authentication create vulnerabilities. Biometric solutions behavioral analytics and hardware tokens enhance security but must be implemented correctly and inclusively. Identity theft enables account takeover transaction fraud and synthetic identities all of which are increasing in sophistication and frequency. Cryptocurrencies and decentralized finance introduce novel risks. While blockchain technologies offer transparency and immutability their implementation can be flawed. Smart contract vulnerabilities insecure wallets phishing schemes rug pulls and exchange breaches have cost users billions of dollars. The pseudonymous nature of blockchain transactions complicates attribution and recovery. Regulatory ambiguity and inconsistent enforcement further exacerbate the risk. Regulators are responding with new frameworks to ensure safety without stifling innovation. Requirements for anti-money laundering know-your-customer procedures cybersecurity audits and consumer protections are becoming standard. Compliance challenges vary across jurisdictions but the need for harmonized regulation is clear. Financial markets are global and fragmented rules create arbitrage opportunities for criminals and compliance challenges for innovators.

Artificial intelligence in financial systems brings both defensive power and exploitable vulnerabilities. AI models detect fraud monitor transactions automate credit decisions and personalize financial services. However adversarial inputs data poisoning and opaque decision-making introduce risks. Algorithms can unintentionally discriminate amplify bias or be manipulated through model inversion attacks. Responsible AI governance including explainability fairness and oversight is critical. Mobile platforms dominate financial engagement especially in emerging markets. Mobile banking apps peer-to-peer payments and digital wallets provide essential services to underserved populations. However mobile devices are frequently targeted by malware SIM swapping phishing and device theft. Securing mobile endpoints requires encryption app sandboxing secure code development and user education.

Cybercriminals exploit the speed and volume of financial transactions. Business email compromise social engineering fake invoices and insider collusion enable large-scale theft. Attackers often launder funds through cryptocurrencies or use mule accounts to obscure trails. Financial institutions must implement transaction monitoring behavioral analytics and real-time fraud detection. Collaboration across institutions and jurisdictions is necessary to track and disrupt criminal networks. Customer awareness is both a necessity and a challenge. Many users lack understanding of digital risks or how to protect themselves. Financial platforms must provide clear guidance intuitive security controls responsive support and rapid fraud resolution. Building trust requires user empowerment not just technology. Inclusive design ensures that security measures do not exclude vulnerable or less tech-savvy users.Incident response in fintech must be swift and customer-centric. Delays in detecting or responding to breaches can result in large financial losses regulatory penalties and reputational damage. Institutions must prepare for scenarios involving insider threats data leaks credential stuffing and API abuse. Recovery must include forensic analysis notification remediation and strategic communication. Maintaining confidence requires visible competence. Cyber insurance in the financial sector is becoming standard. Policies cover fraud business interruption data breach costs and regulatory fines. However premiums are rising coverage is tightening and exclusions are expanding. Institutions must demonstrate strong controls regular testing and transparent reporting to qualify. Insurance is not a replacement for security but a complement to it. The future of fintech security depends on agility collaboration and innovation. As new platforms emerge defenders must adapt. As criminals evolve institutions must anticipate. Regulation must balance protection with freedom. Technology must serve the public interest. Financial systems are not just about capital they are about confidence. Security ensures that confidence is earned and maintained.

Navigating Cybersecurity in the Era of Smart Cities

Smart cities represent the next evolution of urban life where digital technologies enhance efficiency sustainability and quality of life. From traffic optimization to energy management from surveillance to waste collection from connected infrastructure to citizen services smart cities depend on data and connectivity to function. However the very technologies that make cities smart also introduce new vectors for cyber threats. The security of smart cities is not only about protecting data it is about protecting people systems environments and the urban future.

Smart city ecosystems are composed of interconnected components including Internet of Things devices data analytics platforms cloud infrastructure mobile applications and human interfaces. Sensors monitor traffic cameras detect crime smart meters manage energy autonomous vehicles navigate roads and apps deliver services. These systems rely on continuous communication often over wireless networks using diverse protocols and vendors. A vulnerability in any component can affect the entire system. Privacy concerns are paramount. Smart cities collect massive volumes of data including location biometrics behavioral patterns and personal identifiers. This data enables innovation but also creates surveillance risks. Who controls the data how is it stored who has access and how is it protected These questions demand clear answers. Ethical governance legal frameworks and privacy-preserving technologies such as anonymization and differential privacy must be central to design. IoT devices in smart cities are often vulnerable. Many have limited processing power use outdated firmware lack encryption or default credentials and cannot be updated remotely. These devices are deployed in public spaces attached to infrastructure and operate continuously. Compromising a single device can provide attackers with network access footholds or data leakage. Device authentication secure boot encrypted communication and centralized management are essential controls. Resilience must be built into urban systems. A cyberattack on traffic lights can cause accidents a breach in energy management can trigger blackouts a failure in emergency communication can paralyze response efforts. Redundancy fail-safes manual overrides and cross-sector coordination are required. Critical functions must be prioritized and tested under stress. Risk assessments should consider both cyber and physical consequences. Citizen engagement enhances security. Informed citizens report issues avoid risky behaviors and understand the boundaries of technology. Transparent policies public consultations and inclusive design ensure that technologies serve communities. Security must not be imposed it must be co-created. Inclusion avoids marginalization and promotes trust. Supply chain integrity is vital. Cities procure technology from numerous vendors with varying standards. Weaknesses in components software or maintenance can be exploited. Procurement policies must include cybersecurity requirements life-cycle support and vendor accountability. Open standards and interoperability reduce complexity and increase control. Governance is a cornerstone of secure smart cities. Leadership must establish cybersecurity roles policies budgets and metrics. Coordination across departments utilities service providers and emergency responders is essential. A citywide cybersecurity strategy aligns priorities ensures resource allocation and drives accountability. Public-private partnerships expand capability and enhance resilience.

Smart cities face novel attack scenarios. Attackers may target sensors to manipulate data create traffic chaos disable utilities or cause panic. Ransomware may lock access to systems surveillance data may be leaked or manipulated autonomous systems may be hijacked. Scenario planning tabletop exercises and cyber-physical simulations prepare for these risks. Insurance incident response playbooks and legal protocols complete the defense. Technology vendors must be held to high standards. Secure development processes vulnerability disclosure programs continuous updates and strong customer support are minimum expectations. Cities must evaluate vendors not only by price but by security history ethics and responsiveness. Long-term relationships and shared values promote sustainability. Smart cities must not only be connected they must be secure. The promise of urban transformation depends on the integrity of the systems that enable it.

Chapter Six

The Rise of Cyber Warfare and Nation-State Threats

Cyber warfare has emerged as a defining threat of the twenty-first century reshaping how conflicts are initiated how power is projected and how vulnerabilities are exploited. Unlike traditional warfare which involves physical territories weapons and armed forces cyber warfare occurs in a largely invisible realm where code replaces bullets where servers become battlegrounds and where espionage sabotage and influence are executed with precision and plausible deniability. Nation-state threats have escalated in sophistication frequency and strategic impact challenging not only national security but also global stability corporate integrity and individual freedoms. Nation-states engage in cyber operations for various objectives including espionage disruption propaganda intellectual property theft economic manipulation and prepositioning for future conflicts. These operations may target governments critical infrastructure corporations media organizations or even individual citizens. The appeal of cyber warfare lies in its asymmetry a small group of elite hackers backed by a nation-state can cause massive disruption with limited resources. Cyberattacks offer the ability to strike without crossing borders avoid attribution and shape geopolitical narratives with minimal cost and risk. Advanced Persistent Threat groups often abbreviated as APTs represent the operational arms of nation-state cyber programs. These groups are typically affiliated with or directly controlled by military intelligence or security services and operate with defined missions long timelines and significant resources. They infiltrate networks silently maintain persistent access and exfiltrate data slowly and stealthily. Attribution of their activities requires deep analysis including malware signatures infrastructure links and behavioral patterns. Even when attribution is possible public disclosure is a calculated decision involving diplomatic legal and strategic considerations.

Examples of nation-state cyber operations are no longer hypothetical. Real-world incidents have demonstrated the devastating potential of these capabilities. The Stuxnet worm which targeted Iran's nuclear centrifuges marked the first known instance of cyber weapons causing physical destruction. This operation involved custom malware multiple zero-day exploits and deep knowledge of industrial systems. It set a precedent for future operations blurring the line between cyber and kinetic warfare. Similarly the attacks on Ukraine's power grid by suspected Russian actors highlighted how cyber operations can disable national infrastructure during periods of conflict. China has been associated with widespread cyber espionage campaigns targeting intellectual property sensitive commercial data and strategic government information. Operations such as APT10 and Hafnium have compromised cloud providers industrial firms and research institutions often using supply chain vulnerabilities to gain indirect access. The goal of such campaigns is not immediate disruption but long-term strategic advantage in technological economic and military domains. North Korea has developed cyber capabilities to compensate for conventional military limitations and economic isolation. Their operations have focused on financial theft disruption and influence. The Lazarus Group is linked to attacks on banks cryptocurrency exchanges and the infamous WannaCry ransomware which affected hundreds of thousands of systems globally. These activities fund state operations circumvent sanctions and signal technological prowess. Iranian cyber units have demonstrated growing sophistication focusing on regional adversaries critical infrastructure and influence campaigns. They have conducted operations against water facilities oil companies and industrial networks often using spear-phishing social engineering and wiper malware. These campaigns show the integration of cyber tactics into broader geopolitical strategy including retaliation deterrence and signaling. The United States and its allies maintain robust cyber capabilities both defensive and offensive.

The U.S. Cyber Command for instance operates under a doctrine of persistent engagement aiming to disrupt adversary operations before they can cause harm. Offensive operations are often classified but reports indicate their use against terrorist networks election interference infrastructure manipulation and ransomware groups. Allies such as the United Kingdom Australia and Israel contribute significant capabilities to collective security efforts.

Cyber warfare also involves influence operations targeting public opinion electoral integrity and social cohesion. Nation-states use fake accounts bots deepfakes and coordinated messaging to manipulate narratives spread disinformation and polarize societies. These operations exploit the openness of democratic systems the speed of digital communication and the psychology of human belief. The objective is not just to misinform but to create confusion mistrust and paralysis. Preparation and resilience are key to countering nation-state threats. Governments must develop national cybersecurity strategies invest in talent and infrastructure strengthen critical sectors and collaborate with private industry. Intelligence sharing public-private partnerships tabletop exercises and international cooperation enhance readiness. The integration of cyber defense into military doctrine national planning and diplomacy reflects its central role in modern security. Global norms and diplomacy offer a path toward stability. Initiatives such as the United Nations Group of Governmental Experts the Paris Call for Trust and Security in Cyberspace and bilateral agreements seek to establish boundaries promote transparency and reduce the risk of conflict. However enforcement remains a challenge and geopolitical rivalries often limit progress. Cyber warfare is not science fiction it is a present reality with consequences for peace prosperity and freedom. It redefines power competition and conflict in the digital age. Nations must act with urgency clarity and responsibility to navigate this domain. The future of international stability may depend on how we manage conflict in cyberspace.

Protecting intellectual Property in a Global Digital Market

Protecting intellectual property in the global digital market involves defending the digital assets that represent a company's innovation and competitive advantage. These assets include trade secrets, proprietary algorithms, engineering blueprints, patented inventions, product designs, marketing strategies, and copyrighted content. In the digital age, all of this valuable intellectual property is stored electronically, often shared across networks, devices, and even international borders, which increases its exposure to cyber threats. Cybercriminals and state-sponsored attackers deliberately target this type of information to steal innovations, sabotage development efforts, or give their own industries a shortcut to market advantage. This type of attack is quiet, persistent, and often hard to detect because it doesn't always involve the destruction of data but its unauthorized duplication and misuse.

Organizations face additional challenges when their supply chains or development teams involve overseas partners. Different countries have different laws regarding the enforcement of intellectual property rights, and some regions may lack strong legal frameworks or may even tolerate IP theft if it benefits their national industries. This puts global businesses in a vulnerable position when it comes to protecting their designs, source code, or confidential research once it crosses jurisdictional lines. To protect intellectual property effectively, organizations must combine legal strategies with strong cybersecurity measures. Legal strategies include patenting inventions, registering trademarks, maintaining detailed documentation of creation timelines, and signing non-disclosure agreements with all third parties. Cybersecurity strategies include using encryption to protect data at rest and in transit, limiting access to IP files only to essential personnel, monitoring access logs, implementing intrusion detection systems, and deploying digital rights management tools to control how digital files are used and shared. Organizations must also be cautious with open-source software, which may contain unverified code or hidden vulnerabilities that can be exploited to access proprietary systems. Cloud services, if misconfigured, can also expose valuable intellectual property to the internet. The use of artificial intelligence and machine learning systems introduces a new dimension, where even trained models can sometimes reveal underlying data or proprietary patterns if they're not secured properly. Government support is crucial in this area. National policies that promote innovation must also support IP enforcement. Bilateral agreements and international trade rules should provide businesses with ways to seek redress if their IP is stolen abroad. Agencies focused on intellectual property and cybercrime need to coordinate so investigations can cross borders and evidence can be preserved and used in court.

The protection of intellectual property in cyberspace is not just about preserving legal rights. It is about protecting a company's future, its investments, and its ability to innovate safely in a competitive world. In the wrong hands, stolen IP can erode a business's market edge, damage its reputation, or even be turned into tools that directly compete against the original creator. That's why intellectual property security must be viewed not only as a legal priority but as an integral part of every organization's cybersecurity framework.

The Psychology of Cybersecurity and Human Vulnerabilities

The dual forces of digital globalization and hyper-connectivity have revolutionized how intellectual property is created shared and stolen. In today's economy intellectual property constitutes the core value of many organizations encompassing proprietary algorithms confidential designs trade secrets innovative processes source code research findings marketing strategies and business plans. As businesses expand across borders leverage remote workforces and store data in the cloud intellectual property becomes increasingly exposed. Its protection is not only a business priority but also a matter of national competitiveness and innovation sovereignty.

Cyber threats to intellectual property are varied and persistent. Nation-state actors seek to accelerate domestic advancement by stealing foreign innovations. Competitors engage in corporate espionage to undercut pricing models or leapfrog research cycles. Insider threats including disgruntled employees negligent staff and compromised contractors can exfiltrate critical assets without triggering alarms. Supply chain compromises allow attackers to inject themselves into workflows and extract data at scale.

The human mind is an immensely powerful yet imperfect system. It seeks patterns takes cognitive shortcuts and operates under emotional influences. These traits which support fast and adaptive decision-making in many real-world environments often backfire in cyberspace. Attackers understand these psychological tendencies with alarming precision and use them as primary weapons in social engineering attacks. The evolution of cybersecurity has demonstrated that no matter how strong technical defenses become the human element remains the most consistently exploited vulnerability. A deeper exploration of human psychology reveals how unconscious biases influence digital behavior and security-related decisions. For example confirmation bias leads individuals to trust information that supports what they already believe making them more susceptible to phishing emails that mimic familiar communication styles or known organizations. Optimism bias causes people to believe that they are less likely to be targeted by cybercriminals which in turn reduces their motivation to take security precautions. This false sense of immunity opens doors for attacks that rely on complacency and assumption. Anchoring bias affects how people judge the credibility of a request based on the first piece of information they receive. In credential theft scams attackers exploit this bias by presenting partial information that seems legitimate thereby increasing trust in the rest of the message.

Cognitive load also plays a significant role in vulnerability. When individuals are mentally overloaded due to multitasking stress or information fatigue they are more likely to make impulsive or careless decisions. Cyber attackers exploit these moments by introducing distractions urgency or time constraints to reduce critical thinking. For example messages that pressure a user to act within minutes to avoid account suspension or financial loss bypass deliberate scrutiny. Research shows that even trained individuals fall for these tactics under the right cognitive and emotional conditions. Therefore understanding and reducing cognitive load in digital environments is a core aspect of behavioral cybersecurity design. Memory limitations compound the problem. People struggle to remember complex passwords or security procedures and often resort to insecure behaviors such as reusing passwords across platforms or writing them down in accessible locations. When password requirements are strict and unintuitive users tend to create predictable variations making them easier to guess or crack. The psychological discomfort of remembering multiple security credentials leads users to prioritize convenience over protection especially in non-work settings where they feel less accountable.

Habituation is another psychological factor exploited by cyber adversaries. Repeated exposure to security warnings such as software update prompts or certificate errors leads users to ignore or dismiss them without proper evaluation. Over time users become desensitized to these cues especially if previous encounters resulted in no negative outcomes. The brain adapts by treating the warning as background noise. This habituation significantly undermines the effectiveness of alert systems designed to prevent security breaches. Counteracting this effect requires strategic variation in the design of warnings as well as contextual relevance and timeliness.

Emotional manipulation is a powerful tool in the arsenal of cyber attackers. Emotions like fear greed curiosity urgency and sympathy can override rational judgment. Phishing campaigns that appeal to emotional triggers have significantly higher success rates. An email claiming a loved one is in danger or that a rare financial opportunity is about to expire forces individuals into emotionally charged decision-making. In these moments the amygdala the brain's emotional response center can override the prefrontal cortex where logical reasoning occurs. This neurological response highlights why emotional regulation and mindfulness training can be valuable components of cybersecurity education. Social influence and conformity also play major roles in digital risk behavior. People tend to mimic the behaviors of peers especially in unfamiliar or ambiguous situations. If coworkers routinely ignore software update notifications or bypass multi-factor authentication it normalizes risky behaviors across the organization. Social proof is particularly dangerous in phishing attacks that impersonate internal personnel or IT administrators. Messages that appear to come from authority figures trigger obedience responses especially when phrased with directive language. This psychological phenomenon explains why attackers often spoof organizational hierarchies to enhance compliance among targets. The concept of learned helplessness is especially dangerous in the realm of cybersecurity. When users feel that their actions have little impact on security outcomes or that breaches are inevitable they begin to disengage from protective behaviors. This attitude is compounded by overwhelming security protocols confusing policies and lack of feedback on the effectiveness of their actions. To combat learned helplessness organizations must create user-centric security experiences that are intuitive provide positive reinforcement and clearly demonstrate the value of secure behaviors. Empowerment through education and accessible support channels can reverse apathy and build confidence.

Temporal discounting is another factor that explains poor cybersecurity decisions. People tend to undervalue future risks compared to immediate convenience. This bias leads individuals to postpone software updates ignore security reminders or delay password changes despite knowing the long-term risks. The tendency to favor short-term ease over long-term safety is deeply embedded in human psychology and must be addressed through behavioral nudges reminders and incentive structures that reward proactive actions. The environment in which digital decisions are made also shapes behavior. Environmental design or choice architecture influences how users respond to security prompts. For instance placing the default option on the secure path such as enabling multi-factor authentication by default increases adoption rates. Reducing the number of steps required to perform a secure action or providing clear and simple explanations for why an action is necessary improves compliance. Behavioral economists have long advocated for systems that guide rather than force users toward better choices using gentle nudges instead of punitive constraints.

Trust is another psychological construct that underpins cybersecurity behavior. Humans rely on heuristics or mental shortcuts to determine trustworthiness based on appearance familiarity or prior experience. Cyber attackers manipulate trust by mimicking visual elements logos or writing styles associated with legitimate institutions. Once established trust can be exploited repeatedly which explains why some phishing attacks succeed over extended periods with minimal variation. Rebuilding lost trust after a breach is a complex process requiring transparency accountability and consistent protective behavior from the affected institution. Dual process theory offers another lens through which cybersecurity decisions can be examined. This theory posits that humans operate under two systems of thought. System one is fast intuitive and automatic while system two is slow deliberative and logical. Most digital behaviors including clicking links opening attachments and responding to prompts are governed by system one. Cybersecurity training must therefore shift from relying solely on system two strategies such as policy memorization to engaging system one through habits pattern recognition and automatic secure behavior reinforcement. Habit formation is crucial because it embeds security into subconscious routines rather than relying on conscious effort. Gamification techniques are being explored as a method to reinforce cybersecurity habits by engaging users emotionally and cognitively. These techniques use elements such as points rewards challenges and social comparison to create motivation and sustained engagement. For example users might earn recognition for completing security trainings identifying phishing attempts or using strong passwords. By tapping into intrinsic motivators such as competition mastery and status gamification transforms cybersecurity from a compliance burden into an interactive experience.

Generational and cultural differences also influence susceptibility to cybersecurity threats and responses to training. Younger digital natives may be more comfortable navigating technology but also more likely to assume invincibility. Older users may struggle with interface complexity and become targets for scams exploiting unfamiliarity. Cultural attitudes toward authority privacy and risk affect how individuals approach digital security. Effective awareness programs must be tailored to diverse demographic profiles recognizing that a one-size-fits-all approach will leave significant gaps. The psychological contract between employees and their organizations influences internal cybersecurity posture.

Employees who feel valued respected and involved are more likely to adhere to policies and report suspicious activity. Conversely those who feel disconnected or micromanaged may resist controls or engage in negligent behavior. This highlights the importance of organizational culture in shaping security behavior. Building a positive environment where security is framed as a shared responsibility rather than a punitive mandate creates stronger internal defenses.

Narrative persuasion is another underutilized psychological tool in cybersecurity awareness. Humans are wired to respond to stories more deeply than abstract instructions or statistics. Case studies of breaches personal accounts of victim experiences and fictionalized scenarios can make risks tangible and emotionally resonant. Stories that involve relatable characters real-world consequences and clear moral arcs have been shown to improve memory retention and motivation to act. Integrating narrative elements into training materials increases their impact and reduces the cognitive distance between the user and the threat. The emergence of artificial intelligence in cybersecurity presents both opportunities and challenges for psychological alignment. AI systems can personalize security prompts adjust difficulty levels based on user behavior and provide real-time coaching. However if not carefully designed these systems may erode user agency or increase dependence on automation. Striking a balance between assistance and autonomy is essential to maintaining user engagement and situational awareness.

Feedback loops are essential in shaping secure behavior. Users must be given immediate and relevant feedback about their actions whether positive or corrective. For example when a user successfully identifies a phishing email the system could provide acknowledgment and reinforcement. If a risky behavior is detected the system might offer a brief explanation of the potential consequence and a safer alternative. These micro-interactions build a learning environment that evolves with the user reinforcing positive habits over time. Finally ongoing measurement and research are critical to understanding the changing landscape of human vulnerabilities in cybersecurity. Behavioral metrics such as click-through rates on simulated phishing tests response times to warnings and engagement with training programs offer insight into the effectiveness of interventions. Psychometric assessments can evaluate risk perception decision-making styles and resilience. These data points guide continuous improvement and support the development of evidence-based strategies that align with how people actually think and behave in digital contexts.

In summary the psychology of cybersecurity is a rich complex field that intersects with cognition emotion motivation culture and behavior. As technology evolves so too must our understanding of the human mind in digital environments. By leveraging insights from behavioral science organizations can build more resilient systems more effective training programs and more supportive cultures that address human vulnerabilities not as flaws to be punished but as challenges to be understood and mitigated with empathy precision and innovation.

Chapter Seven

Cybersecurity in the Age of Artificial Intelligence

Artificial intelligence has become one of the most transformative technologies shaping the modern digital landscape. Its applications span data analytics natural language processing automation threat detection and predictive security. However the integration of AI into cybersecurity presents both unprecedented opportunities and novel risks. AI systems can enhance defense capabilities by automating responses analyzing massive datasets and identifying subtle patterns that evade human analysts. Yet attackers also employ AI to develop sophisticated malware evade detection automate phishing campaigns and exploit system vulnerabilities dynamically.

The use of machine learning algorithms allows security systems to detect anomalies in network traffic user behavior and system performance. AI-powered security tools can adapt to evolving threats learning from historical attacks and improving detection accuracy over time. For instance behavioral analytics can identify insider threats by recognizing deviations from normal activities. Similarly AI enhances vulnerability management by prioritizing patching efforts based on exploit likelihood and potential impact. Natural language processing enables automated analysis of unstructured threat intelligence reports social media feeds and dark web chatter providing real-time situational awareness. AI-driven chatbots assist in incident response workflows guiding analysts through investigation steps and remediation procedures. Predictive analytics forecast emerging threats and recommend proactive measures. These capabilities significantly increase the speed and effectiveness of cybersecurity operations. However reliance on AI introduces new attack surfaces. Adversarial machine learning involves manipulating input data to deceive AI models causing misclassification or evasion. Attackers may poison training datasets injecting malicious samples that degrade model performance. Model inversion attacks can extract sensitive training data revealing confidential information. The opacity of complex AI models challenges interpretability and trust leading to difficulties in validating decisions and ensuring accountability. Automated attack tools powered by AI increase scale and sophistication of cyber threats. Generative models can create highly convincing phishing emails customized to individual targets increasing success rates. Deepfake technology can fabricate audio video or text to manipulate social engineering attacks. AI-driven bots coordinate distributed denial-of-service attacks more efficiently. The arms race between attackers and defenders is accelerating as both sides harness AI capabilities.

Ethical considerations around AI in cybersecurity are significant. Issues of bias fairness transparency and privacy must be addressed to avoid harm and maintain trust. AI systems trained on biased or incomplete data risk perpetuating discrimination or false positives leading to operational inefficiencies. Data governance frameworks and ethical guidelines are essential components of responsible AI deployment. Human expertise remains vital. AI augments but does not replace skilled cybersecurity professionals. Analysts must interpret AI outputs validate alerts and make strategic decisions. Training programs must evolve to include AI literacy and interdisciplinary skills combining computer science psychology law and policy. Collaboration between technologists ethicists and domain experts drives holistic solutions. The future of AI in cybersecurity promises even greater integration with emerging technologies such as quantum computing edge computing and 5G networks. These advances will reshape threat landscapes and defense architectures requiring continuous innovation and adaptation. Policymakers regulators and industry leaders must collaborate to foster safe responsible and effective AI use protecting privacy security and human rights.

Building Resilient Cybersecurity Architectures for the Future

The complexity and scale of modern digital ecosystems demand resilient cybersecurity architectures capable of withstanding sophisticated attacks minimizing damage and recovering swiftly. Resilience in cybersecurity refers to the ability of systems organizations and societies to prepare for cyber incidents respond effectively mitigate impacts and restore normal operations. Building resilience requires a holistic approach encompassing technology processes people and governance. Fundamental to resilient architectures is the principle of defense in depth. Multiple layers of protection prevent single points of failure and slow attacker progress. These layers include perimeter security firewalls intrusion detection systems endpoint protection encryption and secure application development. Segmentation limits lateral movement while continuous monitoring enables early detection. Redundancy ensures alternative pathways and backup capabilities to maintain critical functions. Zero trust architecture represents a paradigm shift in resilience design. It assumes no implicit trust within or outside the network requiring strict verification of every access request based on identity device posture and context. This model reduces attack surface and improves visibility. Implementation involves micro-segmentation multi-factor authentication encryption of data in transit and at rest and comprehensive policy enforcement. Resilience also depends on incident response preparedness. Well-defined plans procedures and trained teams are essential. Simulation exercises and tabletop scenarios test capabilities identifying gaps and improving coordination. Rapid containment limits damage while forensic analysis informs remediation and future prevention. Communication strategies maintain stakeholder confidence and regulatory compliance. Automation and orchestration enhance resilience by enabling faster and more consistent response actions. Security orchestration automated response platforms integrate threat intelligence detection tools and response workflows reducing manual burden. AI-driven automation handles repetitive tasks freeing human experts for complex decisions. However automation requires careful configuration and oversight to avoid unintended consequences.

Supply chain resilience is critical as dependencies on third-party vendors and open-source software increase risk exposure. Organizations must assess supplier security posture implement contractual requirements and monitor compliance. Visibility into supply chain components and rapid vulnerability management prevent cascading failures. Collaboration with vendors supports coordinated response and recovery. Cloud computing introduces both resilience opportunities and challenges. Cloud providers offer scalable infrastructure redundancy and disaster recovery options. However shared responsibility models require clients to implement controls appropriate to their environment. Cloud-native security architectures leverage containerization, identity federation, and automated policy enforcement to maintain resilience. Data resilience involves protecting confidentiality integrity and availability. Encryption protects data at rest and in transit while backup and recovery strategies ensure availability. Data classification prioritizes protection efforts based on sensitivity and regulatory requirements. Immutable storage and versioning support recovery from ransomware and accidental deletion. Human factors remain central to resilience. Security awareness training, role-based access controls, and fostering a culture of security support proactive defense and effective incident response. Leadership commitment and resource allocation prioritize resilience initiatives aligning them with organizational goals. Regulatory compliance contributes to resilience by establishing minimum security standards and reporting requirements. Frameworks such as NIST Cybersecurity

Framework ISO 27001 and GDPR provide guidelines and best practices. Compliance audits identify gaps and drive continuous improvement.

Future resilient architectures will integrate emerging technologies such as blockchain for secure transactions distributed ledger for auditability and quantum-resistant cryptography for long-term data protection. The increasing convergence of IT and operational technology requires unified resilience strategies addressing physical and cyber risks.Resilience is not a one-time achievement but an ongoing process of assessment adaptation and improvement. Organizations must anticipate evolving threats leverage innovation and maintain agility to protect assets and ensure mission continuity. Resilient cybersecurity architectures underpin trust in digital systems and enable confident participation in the interconnected world.

Legislative Frameworks and Global Cyber Governance

The rapid evolution of cyber threats and the borderless nature of cyberspace have created an urgent need for robust legislative frameworks and coordinated global governance mechanisms. Cybersecurity law encompasses regulations statutes treaties and standards that govern how digital systems are protected how cybercrimes are prosecuted and how states cooperate to ensure a secure and open internet. Effective legal and governance structures balance security interests with privacy rights, innovation incentives, and human rights protections. At the national level countries have enacted cybersecurity laws addressing data protection breach notification critical infrastructure security cybercrime prevention and incident response. The European Union's General Data Protection Regulation is a landmark framework setting stringent requirements for data privacy, consent, and accountability. The United States has sector-specific laws including HIPAA for healthcare and the Cybersecurity Information Sharing Act encouraging threat intelligence sharing between private and public sectors. Other nations have developed comprehensive cyber laws tailored to their legal systems and threat environments. International cooperation is vital due to the transnational nature of cyber threats. Bilateral and multilateral agreements facilitate information sharing, joint investigations, extradition of cybercriminals, and coordinated responses to large-scale incidents. Organizations such as the United Nations International Telecommunication Union INTERPOL and the Council of Europe play significant roles in shaping norms and promoting dialogue. The Budapest Convention on Cybercrime remains the primary international treaty for harmonizing cybercrime legislation and fostering cooperation.

Challenges to global cyber governance include divergent national interests, varying levels of technological development, legal system differences, and concerns over sovereignty. Authoritarian regimes may resist norms that restrict state control over information. Democracies emphasize openness and human rights, creating tension in consensus building. Cyber arms races and strategic competition complicate trust and transparency efforts. Emerging areas such as regulation of artificial intelligence, data localization laws, and internet governance debates add complexity to the landscape. Policymakers must balance fostering innovation with managing risks and protecting fundamental freedoms. Multistakeholder approaches involving governments, industry, civil society, and academia promote inclusive and adaptive governance.

Enforcement remains a critical challenge. Attribution difficulties complicate legal action against perpetrators. Cybercrime investigations require technical expertise, cross-border cooperation, and timely information exchange. Legal frameworks must evolve to address new modalities such as ransomware, cryptocurrency-facilitated crimes, and supply chain attacks.

Privacy protection and human rights considerations are integral to cybersecurity legislation. Laws must safeguard freedom of expression, protect personal data, and ensure due process. Surveillance measures implemented in the name of security require oversight and accountability to prevent abuse. Transparency and public participation in policymaking build legitimacy and trust. Capacity building and technical assistance support developing countries in establishing effective cybersecurity laws and governance. International aid and partnerships help address disparities in resources, expertise, and infrastructure. Enhancing global cyber resilience requires elevating security standards worldwide. Public-private partnerships bridge gaps between regulatory requirements and operational realities. The private sector owns and operates much of the internet infrastructure and critical services. Collaborative frameworks facilitate information sharing, incident response, and joint development of best practices. Future global governance will likely involve evolving norms for state behavior in cyberspace, cyber arms control agreements, and mechanisms for peaceful dispute resolution. Advances in technology may prompt reconsideration of sovereignty concepts and new forms of digital diplomacy.

In conclusion legislative frameworks and global cyber governance form the foundation of a secure digital environment. They provide rules, incentives, protections, and forums necessary to manage the complex challenges of cybersecurity. Continued dialogue, innovation, and cooperation are essential to adapt to the dynamic cyber landscape and safeguard the benefits of connectivity for all.

Chapter Eight

Emerging Threats in the Quantum Computing Era

Quantum computing is no longer confined to theoretical physics or distant scientific speculation. It is rapidly transitioning from laboratory curiosity to a disruptive force capable of overturning the very foundations of cybersecurity. Unlike classical computers which use bits to represent information in binary states of zero or one quantum computers use quantum bits or qubits which can exist in multiple states simultaneously due to the principles of superposition and entanglement. This parallelism grants quantum machines the potential to solve certain computational problems exponentially faster than any traditional architecture. For cybersecurity this shift represents both an existential threat and a profound call to action.

The core concern in cybersecurity lies with public key cryptography which underpins the secure exchange of information over the internet. Algorithms like RSA Diffie-Hellman and elliptic curve cryptography derive their strength from the computational difficulty of problems such as integer factorization and discrete logarithms. These problems are practically impossible to solve with classical machines within any reasonable timeframe ensuring data protection. However quantum algorithms such as Shor's algorithm directly target these mathematical foundations. When sufficiently powerful quantum computers are realized these cryptosystems will become obsolete as their core problems will be solvable in polynomial time. This threat is not hypothetical. Security experts refer to the harvest now decrypt later strategy in which adversaries collect encrypted data today anticipating that in the future quantum computers will decrypt it instantly. Sensitive records diplomatic communications corporate secrets and personal archives may all be vulnerable. Quantum decryption threatens not only future confidentiality but also retroactive exposure of past secure data. This possibility creates urgency around quantum-safe or post-quantum cryptography. Post-quantum cryptography involves cryptographic algorithms that are believed to be secure against both classical and quantum attacks. Unlike quantum cryptography which relies on quantum mechanics for security post-quantum methods are intended to run on classical computers using problems not easily broken by quantum techniques. The National Institute of Standards and Technology has been leading a multi-year process to evaluate and standardize post-quantum algorithms. Among the finalistsare lattice-based hash-based code-based and multivariate polynomial-based schemes each with unique trade-offs in security size and performance.

Migration to quantum-resistant algorithms is a complex and systemic challenge. Cryptographic infrastructure is deeply embedded in software libraries network protocols operating systems and hardware devices. Replacing or upgrading this infrastructure requires careful planning compatibility testing and coordination across industries and governments. The process will span years and involve billions of devices. Moreover post-quantum algorithms tend to have larger key sizes and longer processing times affecting performance and requiring engineering adaptations. Governments around the world have begun preparing for the quantum era. The United States passed the Quantum Computing Cybersecurity Preparedness Act mandating federal agencies to inventory cryptographic usage and plan for migration. The European Union Japan China and Canada have initiated similar programs including funding for research and public-private collaboration. These efforts aim to maintain national security protect economic interests and ensure technological leadership in a post-quantum world. Quantum computing also presents opportunities for cybersecurity. Quantum key distribution enables the generation of cryptographic keys with provable security based on quantum physics. Any eavesdropping attempt disturbs the quantum state thereby alerting the communicating parties. While promising this technology remains expensive limited in range and challenging to integrate into existing infrastructure. Future innovations may improve its feasibility but for now post-quantum cryptography offers a more scalable defense. The timeline for a practical quantum computer capable of breaking modern encryption remains uncertain. Estimates vary widely depending on technological breakthroughs in qubit stability error correction and scaling. Some predict it may take a decade others suggest it could happen sooner. Regardless of the exact timeline the transition to quantum-safe infrastructure must begin now. Waiting until the threat materializes will be too late.

Businesses must assess their cryptographic exposure prioritize critical systems and implement agility in their security architecture. Crypto-agility refers to the ability to switch cryptographic algorithms and parameters without reengineering entire systems. Agile architectures facilitate phased migration reduce disruption and future-proof applications. Leadership must be engaged budget allocated and migration strategies developed in alignment with evolving standards. Quantum computing will also impact digital signatures which authenticate the origin and integrity of messages. Today's signature schemes will become vulnerable to quantum attacks threatening software updates legal contracts blockchain systems and identity management. Post-quantum signature schemes are thus vital to ensure trust in digital communication and commerce. In summary quantum computing represents both a catastrophic threat to classical cryptography and a transformative force for secure communication. The cybersecurity community must embrace proactive strategies adopt quantum-safe standards and lead a global transition toward resilience. The actions taken today will determine whether the quantum future is secure or exposed. The quantum clock is ticking and cybersecurity must be prepared before it strikes.

Cybersecurity in the Global Supply Chain

Ethical Challenges in the Age of Ubiquitous Surveillance

In an interconnected economy organizations rely on a complex web of suppliers manufacturers logistics providers service contractors software vendors and cloud platforms to function. This global supply chain introduces a vast and often poorly understood set of cybersecurity risks. A single vulnerability in one supplier can cascade through the entire chain exposing multiple entities to compromise data theft and operational disruption. Cybersecurity in the supply chain is no longer a technical concern it is a strategic imperative involving governance risk management and cross-border collaboration. Supply chain attacks exploit the trust placed in third-party providers. By compromising a vendor attackers can insert malicious code into software updates tamper with hardware components or gain privileged access to client networks. The SolarWinds attack remains one of the most high-profile examples where nation-state actors compromised a widely used IT management platform affecting thousands of organizations including government agencies and critical infrastructure. These attacks are stealthy persistent and difficult to detect as they abuse legitimate relationships and authorized access paths.

The challenge lies in visibility and control. Organizations often lack insight into their vendors' security practices infrastructure dependencies or subcontracting arrangements. Fourth and fifth-party risks are common yet unmonitored. The opacity of global supply chains exacerbates this problem particularly when components are sourced from jurisdictions with weak regulations poor oversight or geopolitical adversaries. Risk assessments must extend beyond direct suppliers to map the entire dependency graph. Vendor risk management programs must be formalized and resourced. Security questionnaires audits penetration tests and certifications provide assurance but must be tailored to each supplier's role and exposure. Contracts should include cybersecurity requirements such as encryption standards patching obligations breach notification timelines and right-to-audit clauses. Procurement teams must work alongside security teams to evaluate vendors not just on cost and delivery but on trust and security posture.

Secure software development is crucial. Software supply chain security focuses on ensuring that code dependencies libraries and build environments are not compromised. Practices include signed builds reproducible builds code integrity checks and the use of software bills of materials. The U.S. Executive Order on Improving the Nation's Cybersecurity mandates SBOMs for government vendors setting a precedent for broader adoption. Transparency in software composition enables faster response to vulnerabilities and reduces exposure to hidden threats.Hardware supply chain security introduces physical risks including tampered chips counterfeit components and malicious firmware. Ensuring the provenance of hardware through secure manufacturing trusted foundries tamper-evident packaging and chain-of-custody tracking mitigates these risks. Government programs such as the Trusted Foundry Program and private initiatives in secure semiconductor design aim to address these vulnerabilities. Cloud services and managed service providers present another dimension of supply chain risk. Organizations must evaluate cloud providers' security controls resilience capabilities access management practices and compliance with regulatory standards. Misconfigurations in shared environments can expose sensitive data to unauthorized access. Service Level Agreements must specify security responsibilities and incident response expectations. Incident response in supply chain breaches requires rapid containment vendor coordination forensic analysis and public communication. Trust may be temporarily broken but transparent and competent handling can restore confidence. Organizations must plan for supply chain disruptions as part of their business continuity and disaster recovery strategies. Simulated breach exercises involving vendors increase preparedness and identify gaps.

International cooperation is essential. Supply chains cross borders and no single country can secure them in isolation. Harmonized standards mutual recognition frameworks information sharing and law enforcement collaboration support global resilience. International norms for responsible behavior in cyberspace should include obligations for supply chain integrity. Cyber insurance is increasingly including supply chain clauses but underwriting requires detailed risk data. Insurers may demand visibility into vendor relationships security controls and incident history. Organizations with robust supply chain security can negotiate better terms and coverage. Supply chain resilience includes diversification avoiding single points of failure and developing alternative sourcing strategies. Critical sectors such as healthcare energy defense and finance require special attention. Governments may designate strategic suppliers regulate foreign involvement and invest in domestic capability to reduce systemic risk. In conclusion the global supply chain is both an enabler of innovation and a vector of vulnerability. Cybersecurity must be embedded throughout from procurement to operation to decommissioning. Trust in the digital economy depends on securing the unseen hands that make it work. The proliferation of surveillance technologies in both public and private spheres has created a new set of ethical challenges that intersect directly with cybersecurity. Ubiquitous surveillance refers to the pervasive presence of sensors cameras data collection tools and analytic systems that observe individuals behavior environments and interactions in real time. From facial recognition in public spaces to data tracking on mobile devices from workplace monitoring to smart home devices the ability to surveil has expanded faster than the ability to govern it. This reality demands urgent ethical reflection and policy innovation.

At the heart of the ethical challenge is the tension between security and privacy. Surveillance systems are often justified on grounds of crime prevention national security or operational efficiency. However without clear limits oversight or accountability such systems risk becoming tools of control discrimination and oppression. The collection storage and analysis of personal data must respect individual rights adhere to legal standards and align with societal values. Consent is a foundational principle in data ethics yet is often undermined in practice. Users may be unaware of being monitored or may lack meaningful alternatives. Terms of service are rarely read and even when accepted the implications are not fully understood. In public spaces individuals cannot opt out of camera surveillance. In workplaces employees may face implicit coercion to accept monitoring. Ethical surveillance requires transparency informed consent and respect for autonomy. Data minimization is an essential practice. Collect only what is necessary retain it only as long as needed and protect it rigorously. The principle of proportionality demands that the intrusiveness of surveillance is justified by its purpose. Blanket data collection speculative monitoring and profiling based on vague criteria erode trust and violate ethical norms.

Bias in surveillance technology particularly in facial recognition algorithms has raised major concerns. Studies have shown that these systems often perform poorly on people of color women and non-binary individuals leading to misidentification wrongful arrests and discriminatory outcomes. Algorithmic transparency fairness audits and inclusive training datasets are necessary to mitigate these harms. Ethical AI development must be a prerequisite not an afterthought.

Surveillance in authoritarian regimes demonstrates the dark potential of unchecked monitoring. Mass surveillance enables censorship social control and persecution of dissent. Surveillance capitalism in democratic societies creates another ethical dilemma as corporations collect and monetize vast amounts of user data often without explicit consent. These practices commodify personal experience and distort user agency. Cybersecurity professionals must navigate these ethical landscapes with care. Designing securing and deploying surveillance systems entails responsibility. Threat modeling must include human rights impact. Security architectures must prevent misuse abuse and unauthorized access. Ethical frameworks must be embedded into technology design organizational policies and legal compliance.

Regulators have begun to respond. The European General Data Protection Regulation enshrines principles of privacy by design accountability and user rights. California's Consumer Privacy Act sets similar standards. Emerging laws seek to regulate biometric data AI transparency and surveillance limits. However regulation often lags behind innovation and enforcement varies widely. Ethical leadership is critical. Organizations must establish governance structures to evaluate surveillance practices implement privacy policies train staff and engage stakeholders. Public discourse and democratic deliberation must inform decisions about surveillance scope use and oversight. Trustworthy institutions result from ethical choices not just technical excellence. Education empowers citizens. Understanding data rights privacy tools and surveillance impacts enables informed participation. Schools media and civic institutions must promote digital literacy and ethical awareness. An informed society can demand accountability and shape the ethical contours of technological power.

In closing the age of ubiquitous surveillance is a defining challenge of the digital era. Security without ethics becomes tyranny. Convenience without privacy becomes coercion. Innovation without humanity becomes exploitation. Ethical cybersecurity requires not only protecting systems from attack but protecting individuals from abuse. The true test of our digital future lies in whether we can secure not only our data but our dignity.

Chapter Nine

Securing the Internet of Things in an Expanding Digital Frontier

The Internet of Things has revolutionized the way individuals businesses and governments operate by interconnecting billions of devices across homes factories cities and transportation systems. These devices gather transmit and act on data to enable automation efficiency and real-time decision making. However the sheer scale and heterogeneity of IoT ecosystems introduce unprecedented cybersecurity challenges. Devices often possess limited processing power and memory which restricts their ability to run sophisticated security controls. Many are deployed with default credentials insecure configurations or outdated firmware that expose them to exploitation. The diversity of manufacturers protocols and standards further complicates unified security approaches.

Securing IoT demands a holistic strategy that spans device design manufacturing deployment and lifecycle management. Security must be integrated from the earliest development stages with hardware-based root of trust secure boot processes and tamper-resistant components. Firmware must support regular authenticated updates to patch vulnerabilities promptly. Network segmentation separates IoT traffic from critical infrastructure reducing risk of lateral movement during breaches. Authentication and authorization protocols ensure that only legitimate devices and users access sensitive systems. Encryption protects data both in transit and at rest. Threat modeling tailored to specific IoT use cases helps prioritize defenses against the most relevant risks. Common attack vectors include botnets that conscript IoT devices into distributed denial-of-service campaigns ransomware targeting industrial control systems exploitation of weak wireless protocols and physical tampering. Advanced persistent threats increasingly target critical infrastructure IoT components aiming for long-term disruption or espionage. As the number of connected devices grows expected to reach tens of billions within a few years IoT security will remain a focal point of cybersecurity efforts globally. Industry collaboration on security standards is vital. Frameworks such as the IoT Cybersecurity Improvement Act and guidelines from organizations like the Internet Engineering Task Force provide benchmarks for manufacturers and consumers. Certification programs encourage adherence to best practices building trust in the market. Regulatory bodies are beginning to mandate minimum security requirements for IoT products to safeguard consumers and national security interests.

The integration of artificial intelligence and machine learning with IoT offers opportunities to enhance security by enabling anomaly detection predictive maintenance and automated threat response. However these technologies also introduce new risks if not carefully managed including adversarial attacks against AI models and data poisoning. Privacy concerns arise from pervasive data collection by IoT devices especially those monitoring personal or sensitive environments. Transparency and user control over data use are essential to maintain trust. In conclusion securing the Internet of Things requires comprehensive multi-layered defense strategies technological innovation and cross-sector cooperation. Failure to address IoT vulnerabilities jeopardizes not only individual devices but entire networks and critical services. Protecting this expanding digital frontier is essential to realizing the full benefits of connectivity safely and sustainably.

Cybersecurity in the Era of 5G and Beyond

The rollout of 5G networks heralds a new era in telecommunications with promises of ultra-low latency high bandwidth and massive device connectivity. These advances enable transformative applications such as autonomous vehicles remote surgery augmented reality and smart cities. Yet the complexity and scale of 5G infrastructure present unique cybersecurity challenges requiring innovative solutions. 5G networks rely on software defined networking network function virtualization and cloud-native architectures increasing attack surfaces and dependency on software security. The use of open interfaces and third-party suppliers further complicates supply chain security. Network slicing which allows multiple virtual networks on a shared physical infrastructure must be secured to prevent cross-slice attacks and data leakage.

Securing 5G demands comprehensive approaches spanning identity management encryption endpoint security and continuous monitoring. Zero trust principles are critical in authenticating devices users and network functions. Automated threat detection leveraging AI can help identify and respond to emerging risks in real-time. Collaboration between network operators regulators equipment manufacturers and service providers enhances security posture.

The introduction of 5G expands the threat landscape for Internet of Things devices connected via cellular networks. Attacks targeting IoT endpoints can propagate rapidly affecting critical infrastructure and services. New security protocols must address authentication scalability and resilience of IoT communications over 5G. Privacy considerations intensify with increased data flows and location tracking capabilities enabled by 5G. Strong encryption and data protection regulations are necessary to safeguard user information. Transparency in data handling and user consent remain paramount. Looking beyond 5G emerging technologies such as 6G and quantum networking promise even greater capabilities and new challenges. Preparing cybersecurity frameworks to evolve alongside these technologies ensures ongoing protection of digital ecosystems.

In summary the era of 5G and beyond offers unprecedented opportunities alongside complex cybersecurity demands. Proactive investment in secure network design continuous innovation and multistakeholder cooperation will determine the safety and reliability of next-generation communication networks.

The Future of Cybersecurity Workforce and Skills Development

The escalating complexity of cyber threats and rapid technological change have heightened the demand for a highly skilled cybersecurity workforce. Organizations worldwide face shortages of qualified professionals capable of designing implementing and managing robust security programs. Addressing this skills gap is critical to safeguarding digital assets and infrastructure. The future cybersecurity workforce must possess diverse competencies including technical expertise in areas such as cloud security artificial intelligence cryptography and incident response. Equally important are soft skills like communication critical thinking problem-solving and adaptability. The ability to work collaboratively across disciplines and with non-technical stakeholders enhances overall security effectiveness.

Education and training pathways are evolving to meet these needs. Universities and colleges are expanding specialized cybersecurity programs offering degrees and certifications. Bootcamps and online platforms provide flexible upskilling opportunities. Hands-on experience through labs competitions and internships is vital to bridge theory and practice. Organizations must invest in continuous professional development and career progression to retain talent. Mentorship programs and knowledge sharing communities foster growth and resilience. Diversity and inclusion initiatives broaden participation drawing from underrepresented groups to enrich perspectives and innovation. Automation and AI will transform cybersecurity roles by handling routine tasks such as alert triage and vulnerability scanning freeing professionals to focus on strategic and complex challenges. This shift necessitates ongoing learning to keep pace with technological advancements.

Governments industry and academia must collaborate to develop frameworks supporting workforce development including standardized curricula, certification pathways, and funding for research and education. Public-private partnerships can enhance practical training and create pipelines for talent entry. Ethical considerations are increasingly integrated into cybersecurity education emphasizing responsibility, privacy, and human rights. Building a workforce committed to ethical practices strengthens trust and social license. In conclusion the future cybersecurity workforce is central to navigating evolving threats and enabling digital transformation. Strategic investment in education, skills development, and inclusive culture will build the capacity needed to protect the hyper-connected ecosystem now and into the future.

Chapter Ten

The Role of Cybersecurity in Digital Transformation

Digital transformation has become one of the most significant forces shaping modern enterprises. As organizations strive to leverage emerging technologies to optimize processes, enhance customer experiences, and foster innovation, cybersecurity stands at the heart of this evolution. Digital transformation is not simply the adoption of new tools but a fundamental rethinking of business models, workflows, and interactions. This process involves cloud migration, deployment of artificial intelligence, integration of Internet of Things devices, adoption of mobile platforms, and much more. Each facet introduces new cybersecurity complexities that must be managed proactively to avoid catastrophic failures. Security can no longer be an afterthought or a separate silo within organizations undergoing digital transformation. Instead cybersecurity must be integrated into every stage of the transformation journey, from initial strategy formulation through system design, implementation, and ongoing operations. This approach is often called security by design or secure by default. It ensures that security considerations influence architectural choices, data handling policies, identity and access management, and system interoperability. Organizations adopting DevOps and Agile methodologies are increasingly implementing DevSecOps practices where security is embedded into continuous integration and continuous deployment pipelines, enabling rapid yet secure software delivery. One of the greatest challenges in securing digital transformation lies in the hybrid and multi-cloud environments that enterprises operate. Cloud platforms provide scalability and flexibility but also introduce shared responsibility models, complex identity management, and expanded attack surfaces. Misconfigurations remain a leading cause of data breaches in cloud environments, underscoring the need for automated security monitoring, configuration auditing, and strict access controls. Encryption of data at rest and in transit, key management, and network segmentation are critical controls. Organizations must also adopt zero trust principles where no user or device is inherently trusted regardless of location, reducing risks of lateral movement inside networks. Data is a vital asset driving digital transformation. Organizations collect vast amounts of data from customers, employees, partners, and devices. Protecting data privacy and integrity is paramount to comply with regulations such as the General Data Protection Regulation, the California Consumer Privacy Act, and sector-specific rules like HIPAA. Data governance frameworks establish policies on data classification, retention, access rights, and breach notification.

Privacy enhancing technologies such as anonymization, pseudonymization, and differential privacy are increasingly deployed to allow analytics while minimizing exposure of sensitive information. Transparent data use policies and obtaining informed consent build user trust and promote ethical data stewardship.

Cybersecurity is also central to safeguarding innovation. Intellectual property, proprietary algorithms, and customer insights are valuable digital assets that require rigorous protection throughout digital transformation efforts. Collaboration tools, DevOps pipelines, and cloud development environments must incorporate security controls to prevent leakage or unauthorized modification of intellectual property. Furthermore the rise of software supply chain risks demands thorough vetting of third-party libraries, dependencies, and service providers. Organizations must implement rigorous software bill of materials tracking and continuous monitoring to detect compromised components. The cultural and organizational aspects of cybersecurity during digital transformation cannot be overlooked. Leadership commitment is essential to prioritize security investments, set clear policies, and foster a security-aware culture. Training programs help employees recognize social engineering attempts and adopt secure behaviors. Security and business teams must collaborate closely to balance innovation agility with risk management. Governance structures and metrics enable continuous assessment and improvement of security posture.

However these benefits come with elevated cybersecurity risks that require integrated, comprehensive, and adaptive security strategies. Cybersecurity is a critical enabler of digital transformation success ensuring resilience, trust, and sustainable innovation.

Building Cyber Resilience Through Strategic Risk Management

In today's hyper-connected ecosystem cyber threats are increasingly sophisticated, persistent, and capable of inflicting widespread disruption. Traditional defensive postures focused solely on prevention are no longer sufficient. Organizations must develop cyber resilience, the ability to anticipate, withstand, recover from, and adapt to adverse cyber events. Strategic risk management forms the cornerstone of this resilience, enabling organizations to make informed decisions that balance risk with business objectives.

Effective cyber risk management begins with a comprehensive understanding of the organization's digital assets, attack surface, and threat landscape. Asset inventories should include hardware, software, data repositories, network components, and third-party dependencies. This visibility enables identification of critical assets whose compromise would result in significant operational, financial, or reputational harm. Threat intelligence gathered from open sources, industry sharing groups, and government agencies provides insight into adversary tactics, techniques, and procedures, helping to prioritize risks. Risk assessments leverage both qualitative and quantitative methods to evaluate the likelihood and potential impact of various cyber events. This assessment informs prioritization of security investments, controls implementation, and contingency planning. It is crucial to assess emerging risks such as supply chain vulnerabilities, cloud misconfigurations, insider threats, and zero-day exploits. Regular risk reassessments accommodate the dynamic nature of cyber threats and organizational changes. Governance frameworks formalize accountability and oversight of cybersecurity risk. Executive leadership must view cyber risk as a strategic business issue, allocating resources and setting policies accordingly. Clear roles and responsibilities ensure coordination across IT, security, legal, compliance, and business units. Board-level reporting fosters informed decision-making and risk appetite setting. Compliance with regulatory requirements and industry standards forms an integral part of governance. Cyber resilience extends beyond prevention to include preparation and recovery. Business continuity planning and disaster recovery capabilities must encompass cyber incidents, enabling rapid containment, eradication, and restoration of services. Incident response teams with defined roles and playbooks increase effectiveness. Regular exercises, including simulated cyberattacks, test readiness and uncover gaps. Collaboration with external partners such as law enforcement, cybersecurity firms, and information sharing organizations enhances response capabilities.

Technological solutions augment human efforts. Security Information and Event Management systems aggregate logs and alerts providing real-time visibility. Artificial intelligence and machine learning improve anomaly detection and threat hunting. Automation orchestrates routine response actions accelerating mitigation. However technology must be complemented by skilled analysts, sound processes, and a culture of continuous learning. Supply chain risk management has become a central component of cyber risk strategies. Vulnerabilities in vendors and service providers can cascade across the ecosystem. Organizations must extend risk assessments to third, fourth, and fifth parties, requiring transparency and security assurances. Contractual obligations, audit rights, and ongoing monitoring strengthen supply chain defenses. Diversification and contingency planning reduce reliance on single sources.

In summary building cyber resilience through strategic risk management empowers organizations to transform uncertainty into managed risk. This approach safeguards mission-critical operations, protects stakeholder trust, and enables sustainable growth in an ever-evolving threat environment.

The Future of Privacy in a Hyper-Connected World

Privacy concerns are at the forefront of the digital age as vast quantities of personal data are generated, collected, processed, and shared across hyper-connected environments. The expansion of technologies such as the Internet of Things, artificial intelligence, cloud computing, and big data analytics have amplified both the value and risks associated with personal information. The future of privacy requires a multidimensional approach integrating legal, ethical, technological, and social considerations. Regulatory landscapes have evolved significantly with landmark frameworks like the European Union's General Data Protection Regulation setting global benchmarks. These laws emphasize principles such as data minimization, purpose limitation, transparency, accountability, and individual rights including access, correction, and erasure of data. Organizations must implement privacy by design and by default embedding privacy protections into systems and processes from inception. Compliance requires continuous monitoring, risk assessments, and breach notification mechanisms.

Emerging technologies offer promising solutions for privacy protection. Homomorphic encryption enables data processing on encrypted data without decryption preserving confidentiality. Federated learning allows artificial intelligence models to be trained collaboratively without sharing raw data enhancing privacy. Blockchain technologies provide decentralized control and auditability of data access and transactions empowering individuals. Differential privacy techniques introduce statistical noise to datasets balancing data utility with confidentiality. Balancing privacy with security remains a delicate task. While data sharing and analysis can improve threat detection, personalized services, and public safety, excessive surveillance risks infringing on civil liberties and societal trust. Ethical frameworks that prioritize respect for autonomy, fairness, and justice guide responsible data use. Organizations must ensure informed consent, meaningful user control, and transparent communication about data practices. The proliferation of surveillance technologies in public and private spheres intensifies concerns. Facial recognition, location tracking, behavioral profiling, and biometric monitoring raise questions about consent, bias, misuse, and accountability. The intersection of privacy with issues of equity, discrimination, and human rights demands vigilance and public discourse. Legislation must keep pace with innovation to prevent abuses and empower enforcement.

User education and empowerment are vital to future privacy. Digital literacy programs enable individuals to understand their data rights and the implications of technology use. Privacy-enhancing tools integrated into devices and applications provide practical means for users to control data collection and sharing. Building a culture of privacy awareness supports collective resilience. International cooperation is necessary given the borderless nature of data flows. Harmonizing standards, mutual recognition of regulations, and cross-border enforcement mechanisms strengthen privacy protections. Multistakeholder dialogues involving governments, industry, civil society, and academia foster balanced approaches. Looking ahead privacy will continue to evolve as technologies, laws, and social norms interact. The ability to protect privacy in a hyper-connected world is fundamental to sustaining trust, innovation, and democratic values. Cybersecurity and privacy must advance hand in hand ensuring that technological progress serves humanity with dignity and respect.

www.ingramcontent.com/pod-product-compliance
Lightning Source LLC
Chambersburg PA
CBHW021215250926
51852CB00006B/12
* 9 7 8 9 2 8 2 8 6 4 3 8 8 *